Making Language Matter

The Common Core State Standards provide a clear and consistent framework for public school systems as they develop student learning goals that define the path to readiness for college, careers, and informed citizenship. While each state is developing its own procedures for adoption of the Standards, individual teachers will continue to hold the ultimate responsibility for devising lesson plans and tailoring instruction to meet these benchmarks.

Making Language Matter will help prospective and practicing teachers develop lessons to meet the benchmarks enumerated in the Standards for the English Language Arts categories: language, speaking and listening, writing, and reading. A timely text for literacy education courses, it explores language topics within these categories and suggests pedagogical approaches and activities for use in 9–12 language arts classrooms. Using a linguistics approach to unify the study of all the language arts, it engages readers in learning how to help students make purposeful language choices essential for both academic and workplace success.

Exercises in each chapter are designed to complement language arts concepts commonly introduced in the secondary classroom. Literary and informational texts referred to in the exercises are intended only to illustrate the particular linguistic concept being taught, and thus may be easily substituted by other works of the instructor's own choosing. The exercises cover a variety of activities that ask students to analyze language use in a range of reading, writing, and oral situations, to discuss the implications of this usage, and, finally, to apply the concepts learned to their own use of language. The exercises include questions for teachers to guide in-class discussion. Each chapter concludes with a "Meeting Students Where They Are" exercise that connects the chapter's concepts to students' daily lives and a "Looking to the Future" exercise that explores language used in contexts beyond school.

Deborah J. Vause is Associate Professor of English and Humanities at York College of Pennsylvania.

Julie S. Amberg is Associate Professor of English and Humanities at York College of Pennsylvania.

Making Language Matter

Teaching Resources for Meeting the
English Language Arts Common Core
State Standards in Grades 9–12

Deborah J. Vause
Julie S. Amberg

Routledge
Taylor & Francis Group

NEW YORK AND LONDON

First published 2013
by Routledge
711 Third Avenue, New York, NY 10017

Simultaneously published in the UK
by Routledge
2 Park Square, Milton Park, Abingdon, Oxon OX14 4RN

Routledge is an imprint of the Taylor & Francis Group, an informa business

© 2013 Taylor & Francis

Library of Congress Cataloging in Publication Data
Vause, Deborah J.
Making language matter : teaching resources for meeting the English language arts common core state standards in grades 9–12 / Deborah J. Vause, Julie S. Amberg.
pages cm
Includes bibliographical references and index.
1. Language arts (Secondary)–United States. 2. Language arts (Secondary)–Standards–United States. I. Amberg, Julie S. II. Title.
LB1631.V38 2013
428.0071'2–dc23
2012007395

ISBN: 978–0–415–52799–6 (hbk)
ISBN: 978–0–415–52800–9 (pbk)
ISBN: 978–0–203–11869–6 (ebk)

Typeset in Bembo
by Keystroke, Station Road, Codsall, Wolverhampton

SUSTAINABLE
FORESTRY
INITIATIVE

Certified Sourcing
www.sfiprogram.org
SFI-00555
The SFI label applies to the text stock.

Printed and bound in the United States of America by Walsworth Publishing Company, Marceline, MO.

Contents

Preface

In June, 2010, the National Governors Association Center for Best Practices, in collaboration with the Council of Chief State School Officers, released the Common Core State Standards (CCSS) for English Language Arts and Mathematics. The Standards were intended to provide a clear and consistent national framework for public school systems as they develop student learning goals that define the path to readiness for college, careers, and informed citizenship.

As we write this in early 2012, 46 out of the 50 U.S. states have adopted the Standards, and each of these states is currently developing its own procedures for their implementation. Yet, as the authors of the Standards point out, ultimately the Standards' successful implementation rests with classroom teachers, who hold the responsibility for devising lesson plans and tailoring instruction to meet these benchmarks. Our resource book, *Making Language Matter: Teaching Resources for Meeting the English Language Arts Common Core State Standards in Grades 9–12*, is designed to help teachers as they work to revise their curricula to meet the Common Core English Language Arts (ELA) Standards. For this reason, the book is organized around the four "anchor" categories identified in the ELA Standards: Language, Speaking and Listening, Writing, and Reading. Under each category, the book provides teaching ideas and exercises that instructors may use in the 9–12 language arts classroom.

Making Language Matter argues that using linguistic concepts in the language arts classroom provides a useful approach to addressing many of the benchmarks outlined in the ELA Standards. Linguistics, the scientific study of human language, has contributed immensely to our knowledge and understanding of the history, structures, and uses of language. As professors of Language and Linguistics who teach many Secondary Education-English students, we are aware of the numerous benefits that a foundation in linguistic knowledge gives to both teachers and students as they engage topics in the language arts curriculum.

Research has shown that introducing high school students to linguistic and language concepts helps them to develop competence in language usage because they begin to understand how language works and how to use it appropriately in diverse communicative situations. In addition, using a linguistics approach in the classroom opens up discussions on a variety of language topics relevant to students' lives both in and out of the classroom, including the appropriate use of slang and jargon, attitudes about dialect variation, the purposes of figurative language, and the effects of language policies, such as those concerning censorship. Using a linguistics approach allows students both to achieve the ELA benchmarks and to obtain the knowledge and skills needed for success in college and beyond.

In Chapter 1, the introduction to *Making Language Matter*, we explain the purposes and methods we have used in writing this book, arguing that a linguistic approach in the secondary language arts classroom will encourage students both to analyze and to use language effectively because it bridges the gap between the classroom and the real world. We also suggest that such an approach will help meet the Common Core State Standards, as well as the various state standards common to language arts curricula, such as knowing language conventions, using language effectively for a variety of purposes, recognizing language diversity, reading texts with increased complexity, and analyzing arguments.

In Chapter 2 we begin our discussion of the ELA Standards by examining the Anchor Standards on Language. As the authors of the Standards note, this category actually underlies all other categories, given that language is at the heart of any curriculum. To meet the Language Standards, students must demonstrate knowledge of how language functions in different contexts and of how one makes effective language choices depending on audience and purpose. To help students meet these Standards, the chapter discusses in detail the act of code-switching, the communicative facility that people have when moving from one language community to another. Linguistics research has revealed that making students aware of code-switching strengthens their ability to recognize and adapt their language to the various communities they encounter in school and, eventually, in both college and the work-place.

Chapter 3 focuses on the Anchor Standards for Speaking and Listening, which concern students' ability to analyze and evaluate oral texts, as well as to organize and present their own ideas to listeners. The chapter continues the discussion of language variation and the relationship between language, culture, and identity by focusing on speaking and listening as modes of communication and as integral parts of the language arts curriculum.

Chapter 4 addresses the Anchor Standards on Writing, which mandate that students be able to demonstrate the ability to write in various genres and for various purposes. The chapter discusses the three kinds of writing that the Standards suggest students learn and build on through each successive grade: argumentative, informational, and narrative.

Chapter 5 concerns the Anchor Standards for Reading. Drawing on texts from a range of genres, the chapter explores the literal and figurative ways in which both informational and fictional works express meaning. In addition, using example passages from various classic and contemporary texts, the chapter suggests to teachers ways to investigate how diverse dialects convey character, and thus drive plot and theme. Included in these discussions are recommendations for teachers on how to talk about nonstandard forms of language, such as slang, and their uses.

PEDAGOGICAL FEATURES

Each chapter contains ideas for exercises that are designed to complement language arts concepts commonly introduced in the secondary classroom. Literary and informational texts referred to in the exercises are intended only to illustrate the particular linguistic concept being taught, and thus may be easily substituted by other works of the instructor's own choosing. The exercises cover a variety of activities that ask students to analyze language use in a range of reading, writing, and oral situations, to discuss the implications of this usage, and, finally, to apply the concepts learned to their own use of language. Each exercise includes for the teacher suggested questions to guide in-class discussion. Finally, each chapter concludes with a "Meeting Students Where They Are" exercise that connects the chapter's concepts to students' daily lives and a "Looking to the Future" exercise that explores language used in contexts beyond school. Students should leave high school understanding that language really does matter; effective language use is essential for success in any future career.

ACKNOWLEDGMENTS

We are grateful to the NGA Center for Best Practices (NGA Center) and the Council of Chief State School Officers (CCSSO) for granting a license to publish copyrighted material: *The Common Core State Standards* © Copyright 2010. National Governors Association Center for Best Practices and Council of Chief State School Officers. All rights reserved.

We wish to acknowledge those who have supported us in the writing of this text. First, we thank our many students who have inspired us by their interest in language and linguistics theory and research, and by our discussions with them about the ways in which secondary instructors can employ linguistic concepts in their teaching. Next, we acknowledge with gratitude the financial assistance of the Funding sub-committee of the Faculty Development Committee of York College of Pennsylvania. We also thank our editor, Naomi Silverman, of Routledge, Taylor and Francis Group, for her belief in this project and for her guidance in its production. We are deeply grateful to Professor Jill Anderson who read and critiqued early versions of the Language chapter and who provided us with very useful information about secondary students and their milieu. Finally, we thank our families for their continued support during this project.

Chapter 1

Applying Linguistic Concepts to Meeting the English Language Arts Common Core State Standards in Grades 9–12

Released in June, 2010, the Common Core State Standards (CCSS) were developed through a state-led initiative coordinated by the National Governors Association Center for Best Practices (NGA Center) and the Council of Chief State School Officers (CCSSO). Governors and state commissioners of education from 48 states, 2 territories, and the District of Columbia committed to developing a common core of state standards in English-language arts and mathematics for grades K–12. As specified by CCSSO and NGA, the Standards are (1) research and evidence based, (2) aligned with college and work expectations, (3) rigorous, and (4) internationally benchmarked.

As of publication, 46 states and the District of Columbia have now signed on to the CCSS. A survey of state school superintendents conducted in late 2010 by the Center on Education Policy (2011) found that, while states anticipate that full implementation of the Standards will not occur until 2013, they plan to make changes in professional development/teacher preparation programs starting in 2012 or earlier.

When they were introduced, the CCSS sparked a number of controversies, ranging from debates over the political aims behind their formulation to criticisms of the Standards themselves. Within roughly a year and a half after their introduction, however, 46 of the 50 U.S. states had adopted the Standards and begun determining how to implement them. Such quick action spoke to recognition of the need for educational reform across the country and acceptance specifically of the CCSS goals, if not the process or purposes of their development.

The CCSS are anchored by the College and Career Readiness Standards, whose fulfillment is designed to enable students to achieve success in both college and the work-place after high school graduation. Attached to these Anchor Standards are the Grade Standards, a guide to step-by-step development at each grade level, leading to eventual fulfillment of the overarching Anchor Standards.

At the heart of the CCSS's definition of college and career readiness is its recognition of the skills required to be a literate person in the 21st century. Noting that students eventually will be required to listen, speak, read, write, and use language effectively in college and in the work-place, the Standards set literacy requirements that apply not only to the English Language Arts but also to history/social studies, science, and technical subjects.

The Standards' focus upon the need for multidisciplinary and real-world literacy is seen in the English Language Arts (ELA) Standards. For instance, it is recommended that 70% of student reading should be in nonfiction, including many real-world texts that students will encounter beyond the classroom, such as newspapers, business reports, essays, etc. In addition, the CCSS-ELA suggest that student writing assignments should reach across disciplines so that students become capable of writing in various genres and in a variety of media, from scientific reports to newspaper articles to historical documentaries. This wide-ranging concept of *literacy* means that English language arts teachers must see themselves as essential members of a larger educational team, joining other instructors from across the curriculum to help students become proficient in reading, writing, speaking and listening, and general language skills.

An expected result of this expanded definition of literacy is that students will more readily recognize the relevance of their studies to the real world. While before now students may have been easily able to connect assignments in nonfiction reading, writing, and speaking to the world outside academia, the CCSS-ELA encourage teachers to expand the school–real-world connection for all assignments. By focusing on studying language, the heart of the English language arts, teachers will easily be able to do this. The fiction *Romeo and Juliet*, for instance, is frequently read in high school classrooms because teenagers recognize the emotional conflicts represented in the play in their own lives. This empathetic response helps them identify with the characters and so become more invested in understanding the complexities of political and social tensions represented in the language of the play. But teachers should also think about connecting the language itself, Shakespeare's language, to the language used in the 21st-century United States. How might listeners today recognize potential violence in the language used in a social gathering, for instance? Or how can the spoken word inspire listeners toward a specific action?

This direct focus on language is explicitly stated in the CCSS-ELA because it makes up one of the four anchor categories: Reading, Writing, Speaking and Listening, and Language. The Standards' descriptions in the category of "Language" emphasize knowledge about the nature and usage of language. So, for instance, they suggest that students should understand how language functions in different contexts or how to make effective choices in their own language use for meaning or style. Recognizing the fundamental importance of language and the study of language itself, the authors of the CCSS note that the skills in this category are "inseparable" from using language in reading, writing, speaking, and listening (p. 51). What the CCSS ultimately indicate, then, through their definition of *literacy* and their recognition of the need to learn about language itself, is that language is intimately connected to all of human experience and that the more command students have of their language, the more successful they will be as students, employees, future leaders, and citizens of the world.

LINGUISTICS AND PEDAGOGY

With the ELA Standards' focus upon language across its categories, teachers will find concepts arising out of the academic study of language—Linguistics—useful as they develop their classroom pedagogy. On the surface, linguistics and language arts pedagogy seem to have little to do with each other, perhaps even to hold contradictory perspectives. Language arts teachers in the United States traditionally have been tasked with schooling their students in reading and writing Standard American English (SAE) and so teacher-education programs have usually focused on that single dialect. Linguistics, however, is the systematic study of all language, a broad field of study, with scholars researching many different topics, including language acquisition, language preservation, semantics, language variation, language policies, and many other subdisciplines. (See Figure 1.1.) The discipline requires the scientific approach of gathering data about language actually in use rather than focusing on just one preferred dialect or language variety. And although direct application of linguistic concepts is seen by Education majors specializing in working with English Language Learners, Education majors working toward general certification in the language arts rarely are exposed to the study of general linguistics.

Linguistics research, though, has shaped language arts pedagogy for decades. Practices of teaching grammar, for example, have shifted from a prescriptivist approach to a more holistic study of language in use, as illustrated in Constance Weaver and Jonathan Bush's *Grammar to Enrich and Enhance Writing* (2008). And the many approaches to teaching reading and writing that have been developed over the years, including the "Whole Language" method, "process writing," "writing across the curriculum," and numerous other pedagogical methods have all developed from linguistics research. More recently, research specifically examining the usefulness of employing linguistics in language arts teaching reveals that pedagogy informed by linguistic theory is extremely effective (Freeman and

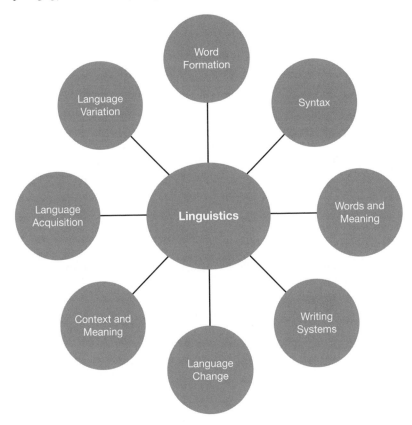

Figure 1.1 Topics within the Discipline of Linguistics

Freeman, 2004; Denham and Lobeck, 2005; Redd and Webb, 2005; Andrews, 2006; Wheeler and Swords, 2006; Hudley and Mallinson, 2010).

As these studies and others have shown, uniting the two fields in the classroom helps students develop their metalinguistic skills, allowing them to understand the reasoning underlying language usage. For example, knowledge of linguistics enables teachers to ground discussions of grammar systems within the understanding of how such systems develop and change over time. This understanding may enrich classroom discussions about why Shakespeare's language is different from contemporary speech, for instance, or why slang is inappropriate in academic discourse.

Knowledge about language can help students make appropriate language choices in diverse communicative situations beyond academe as well, such as in college and the work-place. These situations will require knowing how to use language in many different ways, from using digital tools, to addressing a public audience, to writing a work-place report, reading and summarizing research findings, and so on.

The CCSS-ELA, in fact, build upon a linguistics-based approach, as revealed in its *Appendix A: Research Supporting Key Elements of the Standards* with a specific reference to the need for teachers to have linguistic understanding of language varieties:

> students must be able to communicate effectively in a wide range of print and digital texts, each of which may require different grammatical and usage choices to be effective. *Thus, grammar and usage instruction should acknowledge the many varieties of English that exist and address differences in grammatical structure and usage between these varieties in order to help students make purposeful language choices in their writing and speaking* [italics added].
>
> (p. 29)

Teachers must, therefore, guide students toward a broad linguistic knowledge of language in general, rather than an exclusive focus on SAE. This broader approach will enable students to make the purposeful language choices essential for success in the 21st-century work-place and to understand the language choices made by others in writing, reading, speaking, and listening.

Language and Variation

Perhaps the most visible connection between linguistics and language arts pedagogy to those outside academia lies in the research into American English language variation, which came to national attention in 1977 in the legal case of *Martin Luther King Junior Elementary School Children v. Ann Arbor School District Board*. The verdict in this case declared that teachers have the responsibility of accommodating students who don't use SAE at home. The 15 African American students represented in this lawsuit had been disproportionately placed in remedial and special education classes because teachers had judged them incapable of learning due to their African American English (AAE) dialect use. The court recognized that the school's attitude toward the children's language, rather than the language itself, was handicapping the children's learning. This widely known and important court decision spurred an interest in applying linguistics research to education, especially as it regarded American dialect variation.

One of the results of this interest, roughly twenty years later, was the national debate caused by the Oakland, California school board resolution recognizing "Ebonics," or AAE, as a legitimate language system. Based upon linguistics research demonstrating that dialects were legitimate languages (i.e. rule-governed systems), the Oakland Board had approved the use of AAE in the classroom as a "bridge language," which would help minority students learn SAE. The Board's approval caused an uproar among the general population, however, because the application of linguistics research was misunderstood, an error compounded by inaccurate reporting by the media. Parents of the schoolchildren and others thought that "Ebonics" would be taking the place of SAE in the classroom.

All of the negative media attention in the late 1990s merely fueled research interests so that now, in the 21st century, both primary and secondary educators have a variety of scholarly resources to help them accommodate the range of home dialects students bring into the classroom. Research has moved from focusing almost exclusively on urban students speaking AAE to a much wider range of topics, seen in works like Rebecca Wheeler and Rachel Swords' (2010) *Code-switching Lessons: Grammar Strategies for Linguistically Diverse Writers*, which illustrates the contrastive approach to teaching SAE grammar to students using any American English dialect, and, Anne H. Charity Hudley and Christine Mallinson's (2010) *Understanding English Language Variation in Schools*, which specifically addresses Southern and African American dialects, but also explores how teachers can use their knowledge of language variation to better serve their students in classroom behaviors, assessment, and other pedagogy-related topics.

Language and Success

Knowledge of linguistics has worked in other ways as well to facilitate learning. We can see the intersection of linguistics and education in the other three language arts categories. For instance, the Reading Standards require that students must know about the structure, style, and meaning of texts. Research in the area of linguistics and literature (Early and Ericson, 1993; Janks, 2005) can guide students to this knowledge by having them think about, for example, how context drives language use: depending upon the situation and desired effect, the writer will choose particular words, tone, level of formality, and so on. Concepts that have come out of linguistic research in semantics (Gerbig and Müller-Wood, 2006; Kövecses, 2010) can also help students by encouraging them to consider the purposes and usages of figurative language, not just in literary works but as common occurrences in informational texts and in their own everyday discourse as well.

In the Writing category, students are tasked with knowing how to write in a variety of genres for a wide range of specific purposes. Linguistic theories on genre writing (Devitt, 1993; Wyatt-Smith, 1997; Martin, 2009) have allowed students to develop broad knowledge of genre conventions in an array of rhetorical contexts, thus making them prepared to meet the challenges of any type of writing situation. Finally, linguistics also plays a role in the Speaking and Listening category, with its emphasis upon situating language within context. The Standards in this category ask students to be able to adapt speech to a variety of communicative tasks, altering their word choice, tone, and style depending on the conventions of the rhetorical situation. Linguistics research on discourse and communication (Fodor, 1983; Wheeler, 2005; Brownell, 2009) can aid students in meeting this goal.

Not only should we make our students aware that the study of language is useful to all areas of academe, but we should also encourage them to consider the many ways in which linguistic knowledge relates to the world outside of school. For instance, in many professions it is essential to know how language works: being aware of how names affect consumers' perceptions (the linguistic study of onomastics) is critical to business success; knowing how to defend a student's right to his/her own dialect is essential for achieving teaching success; being able to listen and respond to another's arguments is critical for success in law, commerce, healthcare, service industries, and many other professions.

Finally, linguistic concepts underlie many of the laws and policies that affect students' lives. For instance, in their schools, the policies directing the kind and extent of instruction to English Language Learners, or the guidelines describing appropriate vs. inappropriate grade-level texts are informed by linguistics theory and research. In their non-school lives, they may be asked to join national discussions on issues that many Americans disagree on, such as whether English should be deemed the official language of the United States, or whether federal monies should be spent on the preservation of Native American languages. (See Figure 1.2.) Issues such as these are complex with potential ramifications; the field of linguistics can help our students to approach these issues in systematic and scientific ways in order to be as well-informed as possible.

As the examples above reveal, language plays a central role in many facets of our lives. In order to be informed citizens and successful adults, then, students must be aware of the ways in which language functions both on a micro level within their own personal lives and on a macro level within society as a whole. Instruction that is offered through the prism of linguistics theory and research will aid students in achieving this awareness.

LANGUAGE IN THE NEWS	AT ISSUE
1. Recently, federal workers were warned by the government not to access the WikiLeaks network after WikiLeaks released damaging classified documents. Some workers reported that they had been told their computers would be checked for site activity.	Because the documents had not been declassified, federal employees were asked to apply previously existing policies about classified documents. But since the documents were published publically, this action challenged individuals' right to freedom of inquiry and access to the Internet.
2. In 2011, the small town of Jackson, NY repealed a law passed just one year earlier that designated English as the town's official language because they were warned it could be found discriminatory.	Many towns defend such laws by suggesting that they will help to reduce illegal immigration, as well as illegal hiring of undocumented workers in their municipalities. Opponents point out that legal immigrants and even native-born citizens may not be completely fluent in American English but should have the same rights as others.
3. In 2011, the Supreme Court protected the right of members of the Westboro Baptist Church to picket near a soldier's funeral with signs contending that God was punishing the military for the nation's tolerance of homosexuality.	The Supreme Court ruling protects the First Amendment right of freedom of speech, even hurtful speech, such as in this case.
4. States such as New York and New Jersey are currently debating whether to make it law that hospitals must provide multilingual translators in hospital emergency rooms.	At issue is whether people who do not speak English are receiving unfettered access to healthcare.
5. After receiving a hailstorm of criticism, the LPGA Tour recently backed off a proposed policy that would have suspended players who could not speak English effectively.	Officials proposing the policy point to concerns over the image of the LPGA, while critics of the proposed policy claimed it was "unsportsmanlike" and "un-American."

Figure 1.2 Examples of Language Policies that Impact Voters

Chapter 2

Language

When language arts teachers read through the College and Career Readiness Anchor Standards for Language, they might find fault with the order in which the Standards are listed because they recognize that the listing does not reflect a chronological progression. They know, in fact, that students cannot *demonstrate command of the conventions* of SAE (Standards #1 and #2) without first understanding how *language functions in different contexts* or how they can *make effective choices for meaning and style* (Standard #3). Demonstrating command of language requires knowing its conventions and when to use them. Using SAE, for instance, is appropriate in a courtroom but would be considered snobby and inappropriate if used at a family's holiday celebration. Every communicative context requires a different use of language. First among the skills, then, that students need to learn is the ability to negotiate all language contexts that they encounter.

Language arts teachers know that knowledge about language and, more importantly, the application of such knowledge cannot be conveyed through teaching a few, isolated grammar rules, or engaging students in reading comprehension exercises. Adapting language use so that it's appropriate for different contexts means grasping how language, culture, and identity intersect. For student success in college and beyond, teachers must directly address this intersection in their language arts curricula.

Historically, though, Americans in general have had a limited understanding of how language, culture, and identity work together. For instance, still today, many people consider nonstandard dialects inferior language usage rather than an expression of one's identity and culture. In the past, because of concerns over the way that such an erroneous negative attitude affected student learning, the National Council of Teachers of English (NCTE) endorsed the "Resolution on the Students' Right to Their Own Language." (See www.ncte.org/positions/statements/right toownlanguage.) This resolution, passed in 1974, recognized the dangers inherent in dialect stereotyping and so called on teachers to "expose students to the variety of dialects . . . so that they too will understand the nature of American English," while at the same time affirming that teachers were responsible for teaching students the conventions of "written edited American English." Since 1974, language arts teachers have struggled to follow the NCTE resolution while at the same time meeting the demands of people often untrained in language arts pedagogy, including entities such as local school boards, parent organizations, and others who are concerned with enforcing "correct" language usage for their students. Because of their lack of knowledge about linguistics and the language arts in general, these groups fail to recognize the truth that no one uses SAE all the time and in fact that effective language use means using language appropriately within a given communicative context.

Ironically, all the participants in this struggle over teaching and understanding American English dialects have been motivated by the desire to enable school children to lead successful lives rather than be handicapped by their language use. In his essay, "Pedagogies of the 'Students' Right' Era: The Language Curriculum Research Group's Project for Linguistic Diversity," Scott Wible (2006) traces the conflict between teachers attempting to empower their minority students and the "Back to Basics" educational movement of the 1970s and 1980s that regarded such attempts as lowering expectations and so harming rather than helping the students. He notes that the Oakland Ebonics controversy in 1997 only added to the conflict as it fueled the general public's misunderstanding of language use in the classroom.

More recently, however, research on the value of studying SAE in the classroom by contrasting it with the home dialect of the students has become more widely published (Hazen, 2001; Wheeler, 2002). This chapter pulls from such research by exploring ideas that guide students to analyze the language abilities that they already possess and expand them by adding SAE to their repertoire, rather than focusing exclusively on SAE while excluding any recognition of other dialect use. Thus the chapter begins by establishing a context for understanding all dialect use (Standard #3) and then examines SAE as one, preferred dialect in particular (Standards #1 and #2). The last section of the chapter raises student awareness of how the relationships between words carry meaning, not just the individual words themselves, and so refers to the skills described in Standards #4, #5, and #6. The chapter's ultimate goal is to strengthen the language skills necessary for students to be able to adapt successfully to the varied contexts they will encounter both within and beyond school.

LANGUAGE, IDENTITY, AND COMMUNITY

The first step toward helping students recognize the language abilities they already possess is to make them aware that every individual acquires and uses language in a uniquely personal way. While humans are born with some inherent language acquisition structures, our language development largely depends upon our personal identities, experiences, and education. This notion that language reflects identity is one of the most basic principles of linguistics. As Akmajian, Demers, Farmer, and Harnish (2010) note in a discussion on human language variation, "We are able to recognize different individuals by their distinct speech and language patterns; indeed a person's language is one of the most fundamental features of self-identity" (p. 275). Linguists also recognize that in addition to expressing one's personal identity, language necessarily intertwines with culture—the knowledge, experience, customs, practices, beliefs, and social behaviors of a distinct group of people—and so also reflects the identity of a particular group, or language community. We can see this identity in individual words, such as calling a soft drink "soda" or "pop." (See Table 2.1.) We can also see it in larger uses of language. For example, one language community might shop for "speakers that have a lot of range," while

Table 2.1 Regional Names for Generic Soft Drinks

Name for Soft Drink	Regional Language Communities	Example States
Soda	Northeast	New Hampshire Maine Connecticut
Pop	Central	Iowa Indiana Ohio
Coke	South	North Carolina Georgia Florida
Pop	Northwest	Washington Idaho Oregon

Source: Adapted from Campbell (2003)

another looks for the "premium unlimited 900 MHz wireless indoor-outdoor speakers that include subwoofers." Each community uses language in ways that reflect the needs, interests, and identities of its members.

Standard

3. Apply knowledge of language to understand how language functions in different contexts, to make effective choices for meaning or style, and to comprehend more fully when reading or listening.

EXERCISE 2.1

Have students examine the following list and then note to which language communities they belong. For each community, ask students to jot down typical topics of conversation. What do the members of each group communicate about? What are their interests, concerns, issues, and so on? If communities might talk about the same or similar topics, then in what ways do they converse differently about them? For instance, talk between friends about a school assignment is probably very different from talk between a teacher and a student about that same assignment. Once students have had a chance to consider these communities on their own, ask them to share their individual analyses with the rest of the class.

1. Family
2. Close friends
3. School
4. Work
5. On-line (blog, Twitter, etc.)

Guided Questions for Class Discussion

1. What topics would students discuss with their friends, with family, etc.?
2. Are there topics that they wouldn't discuss in any of these communities? If yes, why wouldn't they? Are there various reasons for avoiding particular topics in some groups? Give students examples of situations where certain topics might not be appropriate, such as discussing their weekend plans with a teacher, or their career plans with a DJ at a club, and so on. How do we know what topic is appropriate in a given situation?
3. How many different school language communities that students belong to can they identify (band, debate club, French club, shop class, etc.)? What makes these language communities different from one another?
4. How did students learn what topics are appropriate and inappropriate for each community?

5. Even if the same topic is discussed in more than one community, do students use exactly the same language? Words? Sentences? Emotional expressions? How does the language use differ?

CODE-SWITCHING

Because each of us belongs to a number of diverse language communities, we possess the ability to *code-switch*, that is, the ability to shift our language to be appropriate for each particular rhetorical situation. (See Table 2.2.) Your own ability to code-switch can be seen in the many different conversations you hold over the course of a single day—those with students, with friends, with a work colleague, with a sales clerk, a neighbor, a spouse, and so on. For example, you might write a grade-level outcomes assessment report during a meeting with colleagues, then teach a freshman language arts class one hour later, and an hour after that place a lunch order in the local deli and joke with friends about "the time when. . . ." Each of these situations demands something different in terms of language to be effective, such as a particular word choice, tone, sentence length, volume, and so on, thus revealing the complexity of the code-switching process.

Students also move among diverse language communities over the course of a day. Helping them to recognize and improve their own ability to code-switch between contexts gives them an important linguistic tool, enabling them to negotiate successfully a variety of rhetorical situations. In addition, recent research (Wheeler, 2002; Hazen, 2001) demonstrates that students' acquisition of SAE can be improved when using a contrastive approach in the classroom, in which different language communities are contrasted and their various languages compared. Wheeler (2005) points out that such a contrastive approach builds on students' own code-switching abilities and has the benefit of empowering all members of a language-diverse classroom.

Table 2.2 Code-switching Between Language Communities

Formal Standard American English	To Young Children	To Grandparents	To Friends
"I'm not feeling very well."	"I feel icky."	"I have a stomach bug."	"I've been barfing all day."
"Sam is my friend."	"Sam's my buddy."	"Sam's my pal."	"Sam's my homie."
"I concur with that sentiment."	"I like what you said."	"We're of the same mind."	"That's legit."

The following exercise provides ways to help students practice a contrastive approach to identify the language conventions of different communities. It is intended to help students become more aware of their own language decisions and thus more able to control those decisions in different contexts.

EXERCISE 2.2

Expanding on their consideration in Exercise 2.1 of typical topics discussed by the language communities they belong to, have students choose one or two language communities from those that they identified above and examine each community's particular language characteristics. Suggest that they consider types of words and phrases, tone, sentence length, and volume used by each community. Table 2.3 provides a guide to help students organize their answers. When students finish their discussion, analyze the results as a class.

Table 2.3 Rubric for Exercise 2.2

	Types of Words and Phrases	Tone	Sentence Length	Volume
Family				
Close friends				
School				
Work				
On-line				

Guided Questions for Class Discussion

1. What makes family (school, work, etc.) language different from school (work, friends, etc.) language?
2. Do different families speak in different ways? Do extended families speak differently than immediate family members? Compare notes among students.

The following exercise gives additional practice to students in identifying language communities.

EXERCISE 2.3

Have students in groups or pairs choose a specific language community scenario and write an 8–10 line dialogue among the participants in the scene. Students can choose from a variety of scenarios, ranging, say, from a parent/child conversation to a police officer/motorist encounter to a boss/worker exchange. Next, have students act out the dialogues in front of the class, letting the other students guess at the participants and their contexts.

Guided Questions for Class Discussion

1. After each skit, ask students to identify the characters being represented. How could they tell?
2. After each skit, ask students to identify and discuss the special language characteristics this community has. What level of formality is used? What types of words? What tones?

The following exercises ask students to apply the concepts learned in the exercises above to non-academic contexts.

Exercise Extension

Ask students to keep a record of all the language communities that they belong to during the course of one day. Then have students write a couple of paragraphs in which they reflect on their ability to code-switch among these communities. Sample questions they might wish to answer in their paragraphs: Was the writer surprised at the number of language communities that he/she belonged to? How do these communities differ? How are they alike?

Exercise Extension

Ask students to write about a time when they consciously attempted to change their language to "fit in" to a specific situation and/or group of people. For example, maybe they were trying to impress a peer(s), or apply for a job, or start at a new school, or keep out of trouble with an authority figure, or another situation. Sample questions they might wish to answer in their writing: What was their motivation in trying to "fit in"? What details do they remember about how they changed their language? Did they use a different vocabulary? Different pronunciation? Different types of sentences (i.e. shorter or longer, more questions, more exclamations, etc.)? And finally, how successful were they in achieving their goal?

Communicative Context

To be able to effectively code-switch, a person not only has to be aware of different communities of speakers, but he or she must know the communicative context as well. If you think for a minute about the differences between the way in which members of a family talk at home to one another and the way they talk to others outside the home, say to a server at a restaurant, it's likely that different words, tones, forms of address, syntax, etc. will be used in each situation. The same individual can employ many different patterns of language usage or registers, depending on the setting and the purpose for the communication. Some might think of language register as a way to acknowledge the level of formality being expressed through a communication, but linguists are much more specific in their use of the term. After all, a variety of language elements conveys formality, ranging from pronunciation to body language to punctuation. Trudgill (1983) perceives register to be a specialized lexicon tied to a socio-professional activity, such as law or medicine. Halliday's (1985) definition of the term, though, illustrates some of the complexities involved in considering register. From his sociolinguistic perspective, a particular communication's register is created by the interaction of three separate factors: the tenor, which is the social roles and relationships of the participants; the mode, which is the medium of the communication; and the field, which is the subject of the communication. So a discussion of register might include vocabulary, syntax, sounds, and even the meaning of a particular communication.

The ability to analyze and understand a communication's context, including register, is crucial for effective communication. This knowledge may sometimes be lacking in high school students, though, since they typically are focused on their peer groups rather than alert to other language contexts. In addition, many students may have experienced little exposure to a variety of communication contexts outside home and school due to socioeconomic or other factors. To be effective communicators in both speech and writing, students need to learn more than just correct and incorrect forms of language. Classroom discussion that focuses on diverse communication contexts will help students make appropriate language choices focusing on their intended purpose with the audience, as well as the language that the audience expects in that particular context. The following exercise continues the contrastive approach by asking students to consider different communication contexts and the language appropriate to each.

Standards

1. Demonstrate command of the conventions of standard English grammar and usage when writing or speaking.
2. Demonstrate command of the conventions of standard English capitalization, punctuation, and spelling when writing.
3. Apply knowledge of language to understand how language functions in different contexts, to make effective choices for meaning or style, and to comprehend more fully when reading or listening.
6. Acquire and use accurately a range of general academic and domain-specific words and phrases sufficient for reading, writing, speaking, and listening at the college and career readiness level; demonstrate independence in gathering vocabulary knowledge when considering a word or phrase important to comprehension or expression.

EXERCISE 2.4

Ask students to analyze each communication context below and, for each situation, identify the language needs for the two contexts listed. Have students consider the purpose of the communication: how much does each audience already know about the topic? What would each audience need to learn about the topic, and why? Then ask students to think about the kind of language appropriate to each audience.

1. Giving a speech on the need for better food in the cafeteria
   a. to the School Board
   b. in front of the student body when running for Student Council office
2. Writing an email asking for help on an assignment
   a. to a teacher
   b. to a friend
3. Writing about a movie
   a. texting to a friend
   b. reviewing in the school newspaper
4. Talking about a concert
   a. to a friend
   b. to the principal of the school

Guided Questions for Class Discussion

1. Ask students what register is required in each situation.
2. How does one make his/her language more or less formal?
3. Have students consider what happens when a listener's or reader's expectations are not met in a language context. For instance, how do students think a friend would react if they used the language normally employed with the principal with that friend, and vice versa?

Drawing on the exercises above that discuss the importance of purpose, context, and audience, the following exercise asks students to analyze how specific elements of language use vary from one rhetorical context to another.

EXERCISE 2.5

Ask students to analyze the four texts below, taken from common communicative contexts, by considering how the language of each is appropriate for its specific audience and purpose. Students will need to consider a broader range of elements than in the previous exercise, expanding their analyses to include topic, format (physical layout of text), word choice, sentence style, and syntax. Table 2.4, a comparison/contrast chart for students to complete, will make this task easier for them.

Table 2.4 Rubric for Exercise 2.5

	Lyrics	Directions	Contract	Newspaper
Purpose of communication				
Intended audience				
Topic				
Format (physical layout)				
Word choice (formal, informal, learned, specialized, spelling, etc.)				
Sentence style (long, short, compound, complex, etc.)				
Syntax (word order in sentences—fragment, question, etc.)				

A. Traditional Children's Song Lyric:
Skip, skip, skip to my Lou,
Skip, skip, skip to my Lou,
Skip, skip, skip to my Lou,
Skip to my Lou, my darlin'.
Fly's in the buttermilk,
Shoo, fly, shoo,
Fly's in the buttermilk,
Shoo, fly, shoo,
Fly's in the buttermilk,
Shoo, fly, shoo,
Skip to my Lou, my darlin'.

B. From *Assembly Directions for a Telescope*:
1. Open the telescope storage box, remove top foam insert. **KEEP YOUR FINGERS CLEAR OF THE WOODEN CRATE WALLS TO AVOID PAINFUL SPLINTERS UNDER NAILS.** . . .
2. Remove the **pier bolt** from the box containing the power supply. Lift the **telescope** out of the box **by the carrying handles** and place it on the pier. . . . **IF YOU HAVE TROUBLE WITH THIS STEP CALL FOR HELP. WE FAR PREFER HELPING YOU LIFT TO PICKING UP DROPPED TELESCOPES!!**
   ("Assembling and Operating Duke's Meade LX200GPS SCT," n.d.)

C. From a standard *Rental Contract*:
ACCEPTANCE OF PROPERTY: Resident accepts the "AS IS" condition of the property, waiving inspection of same by Owner and agrees to notify

Owner of any defects. Resident further agrees to indemnify Owner against any loss or liability arising out of Resident's use of the property, including these using the property with Resident's consent.

D. From "Surging Revs Finally Beat Patriots: York scored its first victory of the season against Somerset with Tuesday's 4–1 triumph":
The Revs won for the eighth time in 10 games and improved to a league-best 11–7 on the road. Third baseman Ramon Castro hit a pair of solo homers.
Castro joined outfielder James Shanks as the only Revs to homer twice in a game this season. And Castro extended his on-base streak to a league-best 26 games. His hitting streak stretched to 11 games—the longest of the season for a York player.

("Surging Revs Finally Beat Patriots," June 2, 2010)

Guided Questions for Class Discussion

1. Formatting provides many helpful cues to knowledgeable readers but may not be something your students have analyzed in much depth. Have your students think about some of the formatting in the passages. Why are some of the sentences in the directions in bold type and in capitals, for instance? Why does the newspaper article have such short paragraphs? And so on. How do the differing purposes, audiences, and subject matters in these specific examples affect formatting? What would happen if writers always used the same format in every writing situation?

2. Ask students to consider the word choices in Examples C and D above. What characterizes the language in Example C? Would these word choices be appropriate in any other context? What metaphors can students identify in Example D? Can students put them into everyday language to explain their meaning?

Perhaps one of the changes in language with which your students will be most familiar is the development of the texting idiom, a written language that has developed only in the past ten or so years. (See Figure 2.1.) Although many consider texting an abbreviated form of SAE, in fact, like any language variation, it has its own grammar conventions, or set of rules. Texting is one way for students to form bonds with others and be part of social networks, and, as such, they may feel a special affinity toward this language variety, that is, they might feel it's the language of their particular peer community. Understanding that texting has its own conventions may help students to recognize yet another instance of their own code-switching abilities, as well as help them match this particular kind of language use to its appropriate context. The following exercise asks students to analyze the conventions of texting.

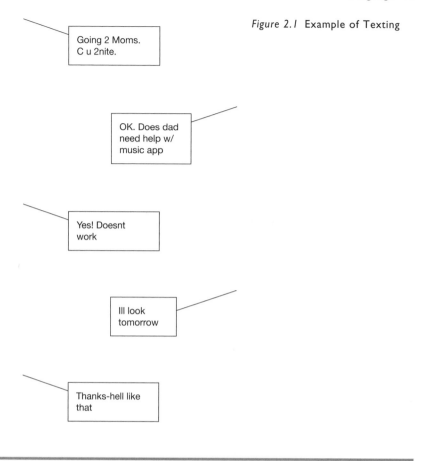

Figure 2.1 Example of Texting

Going 2 Moms.
C u 2nite.

OK. Does dad
need help w/
music app

Yes! Doesnt
work

Ill look
tomorrow

Thanks-hell like
that

EXERCISE 2.6

Bring in examples of text messages that you have collected, perhaps from your own archives, or ask students to bring in samples. Have at least 2–3 full text messages per group so that students will have enough copy to work with. Put students into groups and have them analyze the text messages with the goal of identifying and articulating some rules for the medium. Have them create rules regarding word choice, word spelling, sentence length, sentence structure, tone, and content. For example, must all sentences contain the parts of speech (subject, verb, object) typically considered essential in SAE sentences? How do readers understand the tone? And so on. Once students have created the rules, come back to full class and discuss their lists.

Guided Questions for Class Discussion

1. Ask students what the context is for text messaging. What type of relationship exists between the sender and receiver? What are their motivations for messaging? What kinds of boundaries or limitations are created by this particular electronic medium?

2. Have students consider the kind of content found in text messages. Why this content and not other kinds?

3. What rules did your students discover about word choice and spelling? Sentence length and sentence structure? How might a receiver respond if a sender didn't follow these rules?

4. What aspects of SAE are missing in texting language? How much of a difference does their absence make in terms of comprehension of the message? Why? Why do more formal types of communication include these aspects rather than eliminate them as texting does? (Students should be able to discuss and differentiate among different types of relationships and contexts.) What would happen if one were to use texting language in another context—filling out a job application, for example?

5. What is the tone of most text messages and how does one convey tone? Is it harder to convey tone in texting than in writing in SAE? And why are senders concerned about conveying tone/emotions while texting?

6. Ask students to consider where else in our culture besides on our phones we might see texting. Identify some locations (such as billboards and advertising, spoken conversations, etc.) and then ask students if they think this language usage is appropriate.

ACKNOWLEDGING AMERICAN ENGLISH VARIETIES

Language Variation in the United States

In their discussions of language-appropriate contexts above, you might have heard students declare that some sentence constructions were "better" or more "correct" than others. Their notions about correctness shouldn't be surprising, since at school we tend to test them on their language use, often telling them through grades that their language is wrong or used incorrectly. Because they have been taught to judge language instead of consider its appropriateness in context, many students today, as well as many members of the general public, mistakenly believe that some people speak "better" than others. (See Figure 2.2.)

As you know, for many years professional organizations, such as the NCTE, have worked to correct such mistaken attitudes toward language diversity in the United States. Yet research (Lovejoy, 2003; Wolfram, 2004; Dunn and Lindblom, 2005) has demonstrated the strong link that still exists between people's attitudes toward a dialect, or English variety, and their attitudes toward the people who speak that dialect or variety. Intolerance of a language variety may foster one's negative attitude toward the speaker of that variety, while appreciation of linguistic diversity can lead to acceptance of those different from oneself. Teaching students to understand that the "best" language is always that one that best fits the rhetorical situation will help them to avoid making harmful linguistic, as well as social, stereotypes.

But perhaps even more important to the Language Arts classroom is the linguistic research showing that emphasizing appropriateness rather than correctness is actually more effective in helping students learn SAE than was thought in previous generations (Goodman, 2003; Denham and Lobeck, 2005; Wheeler, 2005). Indeed,

Figure 2.2 Examples of "Bad" Speech?

studies of classroom practices that contrast English varieties (Wolfram, 1993; Hazen, 2001; Wheeler, 2005) have shown that this kind of teaching produces greater student mastery of SAE. As students discuss and compare different varieties of English, they will be able to articulate what they intuitively know as true, that language usage varies, depending on its suitability to the situation. This linguistic approach to language of not judging but, rather, identifying the appropriateness of dialects allows students both to validate the dialects they use and to learn their best usage.

As teachers, we often encounter many different student dialects in one classroom. How do we make sure that students' home language varieties are not deemed "bad" by other students, while at the same time privileging the study of SAE, the dialect targeted for mastery by every state, district, and school language standard? Such a classroom situation can be difficult, but, because the stakes are so high, teachers must consider ways to answer this question. We owe it to our students to teach them the most effective language skills possible. By including discussions on language diversity in lessons on SAE, teachers can help students achieve both the Anchor Standard goals and a greater awareness of our national linguistic heritage and culture.

Standard American English

Everyone in academia knows that one of the most commonly used American English dialects is SAE. The name itself will help students identify the appropriate situations for its use. "Standard" doesn't mean "the best" or most "correct"; instead, it means the general norm—the most widely used and recognized. So when applied to American English, "standard" means that it is the most commonly used or accepted dialect in the United States. Different from other varieties, which are primarily spoken, SAE exists primarily in its written form because it is a learned dialect. No one speaks SAE as their native tongue, yet Americans recognize the vital importance of learning this variety. SAE is the most commonly recognized and understood dialect in the United States, especially within institutional settings, such as in schools, governments, courts, and so on. For students to achieve success in school and beyond, they must know the conventions of SAE.

The importance of learning SAE is reflected in the many benchmarks established in the Anchor Standards that assess students' mastery of its conventions. Yet the Anchor Standards also suggest that students' recognition of the variety of American English dialects is necessary to their becoming critical users of language. Indeed, the Standards note that lessons acknowledging the many varieties of English will help students to make purposeful language choices in their speaking and writing, as well as to understand the choices that others make. For example, Standard #6 of the Anchor Standards for Speaking and Listening recommends that students be able to *adapt speech to a variety of contexts and communicative tasks, demonstrating a command of formal English when indicated or appropriate.* SAE, after all, would not be effective in every kind of written and spoken context. Just think about the way President Obama adapts his language to fit the communicative situation, from answering personal questions asked by the press about his daughters, to making a State of the Union address before Congress. His language changes depending on the context. The following exercise asks students to examine and identify the contexts in which diverse language varieties would be used.

EXERCISE 2.7

Ask students to read the following sentences and identify which of the context choices is appropriate. They might find working with a partner helpful as they consider the topic, word choice, level of emotion, tone, and phrasing. They should be able to explain why the wrong choices are inappropriate, as well as defend their choice for the correct answer.

1. *He don't live here anymore.*
    ___Spoken answer to a question from the teacher in a class
    ___Written answer to a question on a test
    ___Written answer to a survey on the internet
    ___Spoken answer to a question from someone in a local neighborhood
2. *Snowmageddon blankets East Coast.*
    ___Spoken comment at a family dinner
    ___Spoken line in a public official's election speech
    ___Written headline for a news story
    ___Written observation in a meteorologist's monthly report
3. *Jane quickly packed her bag and headed for the train station.*
    ___Spoken comment in a voice message
    ___Spoken answer to a question about Jane's whereabouts
    ___Statement of fact in a history textbook
    ___Written description in a short story
4. *To be successful, Smith Enterprises must meet the following goals:*
    ★Provide superior customer service
    ★Provide quality products
    ★Provide reliable shipping to all parts of the country

___Written entry in a diary
___Spoken observation in a TV news report
___Written section of a business report
___Spoken during a casual conversation between two Smith employees

5. *The standard reagent was used on four samples. Included in the samples was a known constant with a known response. A titration was conducted. The sample from the crime scene showed a positive reaction at .25 cc, thereby confirming it to be the same substance that was taken from the suspect.*
    ___Text message
    ___Written essay on a Spanish test
    ___Conversation about the results of testing
    ___Written section of a lab report

6. *First, set the dial to the desired level of toasting. Then insert a slice of bread into the slot at the top of the toaster. Push down the lever on the front until you hear the click of the spring engaging. Wait a few minutes until the finished toast pops out of the top of the toaster.*
    ___Spoken instructions to a parent
    ___Written directions for using a toaster
    ___Spoken directions to a high school Consumer Science class
    ___Sample paragraph in an ESL textbook

7. *don't u b 18!!!!*
    ___Spoken reminder to a friend
    ___Written sentence in a newspaper article
    ___Written text message to a best friend
    ___Spoken command to a teacher

Guided Questions for Class Discussion

1. What is the tone of the sentence/passage? Formal? Informal? What are the characteristics of formal and informal language? (You may want to list the characteristics on the board as the students come up with ideas.)
2. What are the characteristics of newspaper headlines? Text messaging? (Refer students to the previous exercise if necessary.) Sets of instructions? Scientific prose? Business prose? In addition to considering audience and purpose for each of these genres, ask your students to consider tone, length of sentences, and word choice.
3. Can the students identify some of the major differences between spoken and written language?

WORDS AND WORD RELATIONSHIPS

Effective language use means appropriate language use. The exercises up to this point have focused on using language in the appropriate social context. But we can apply the same concept to individual words within the context of individual sentences. They have to fit, to be appropriate, in order to effectively carry meaning. Language does not use words exclusively in isolation to carry meaning; rather, words are combined with other words to create phrases and clauses that carry meaning as a unit. Linguists who study words and meaning have theorized that humans develop a certain knowledge about word relationships, which they then use to help create meaning (Goddard, 1998; Aitchison, 2003). For instance, certain words set up expectations for others. Consider the sentence *He baked the lasagna for 50 minutes in the oven*. In this case, the verb, *bake*, sets up certain expectations for what is to follow in the rest of the sentence. Listeners or readers have preconceived notions about what can be baked: it must be something inanimate, able to withstand extreme temperatures, and so on. The research shows that humans look at both word meaning and word relationships in context to produce overall meaning.

Standards

4. Determine or clarify the meaning of unknown and multiple-meaning words and phrases by using context clues, analyzing meaningful word parts, and consulting general and specialized reference materials, as appropriate.
5. Demonstrate understanding of figurative language, word relationships, and nuances in word meanings.

EXERCISE 2.8

Building on the concepts discussed above regarding reader/listener expectations when creating meaning, have students read through the following sentences and explain why they are odd. What notions about word meaning and word relationships are students trying to employ to make meaning?

1. *The dog read my book.*
2. *I wandered lonely as a cell phone.*
3. *The girl licked the television.*
4. *Yes, they just finished: they wrapped it into.*
5. *He was racing against the pencil to meet the deadline.*

Guided Questions for Class Discussion

1. Ask your students to describe how their expectations when reading these sentences were variously frustrated and unfulfilled.
2. What makes sentences 4 and 5 different from the first three? Ask students what knowledge they are drawing on both to make meaning and to understand that their expectations aren't being met. You might point out that native speakers of English have an advantage over non-native speakers because of their knowledge of American English idioms.

The following exercise uses a game that you might remember playing in your own teen years. Here we use it to demonstrate the complexities of discourse: for communication to successfully take place, meaning is carried by context, not just by individual words. The humor of this game lies in the inappropriate connections between words and their contexts. Students should be able to quickly see the need to make their own word choices appropriate.

EXERCISE 2.9

The classic Mad Libs game demonstrates the importance of considering conversational context and listeners' needs in order to effectively communicate. To play the game with students, first ask them to write down 2–3 examples for each item requested in the following script (nouns, exclamations, parts of the body, etc.). Next, silently read through the script, asking students to suggest entries from their list of examples for each blank. Choose one suggestion per entry and fill in the blank. Finally, after all the blanks are filled in, read the entire script out loud to students. Note, you may be interested in writing your own scripts, focusing on other contexts that may be particularly familiar to your students: giving a speech in front of class, going to the zoo, talking to the principal, interviewing for a job, visiting Disney World, going to the beach, eating in the cafeteria, and so on. The possible contexts are endless.

Note: This game works best if students do not see the script as the teacher fills in the blanks. Once all the blanks have been filled in and the finished piece read out loud to the class, however, it may be useful to put the script up on an overhead or white board so that students can examine it as they discuss the exercise.

Guided Questions for Class Discussion

1. Why was this dialogue humorous?
2. Given the communicative context, what kind of language did your students expect each of the characters to use? What tone, word choice, gestures, and so on would they expect each to use?
3. Where were the students' expectations not met?
4. Ask students to examine the syntax of each sentence in the Mad Libs text. What words/parts of speech establish expectations for the blank word? For example, what expectation for the word coming next do articles or adjectives create? How do audience members know what tense and number of verb to expect? And so on. Now ask students to explain why the word chosen to fill in the blank clashes with these expectations. And this clash of expectations is, of course, where the humor arises.
5. Invite students to consider the communication going on in this scene: how successful was it?

Sample Script:
"Meeting the Parents"

Tasha felt a little nervous as she got ready for her date. This was going to be the first time that her boyfriend, Dave, was going to meet her _____.
(plural noun—people)

The doorbell _____, and Tasha went to answer it, but her little
(verb)

_____ got there before she did, opened the door, and said,
(sg noun—person)

"_____!" If that wasn't bad enough, her father then
(exclamation)

_____ to the door, reached out his _____,
(verb)   (body part)

and asked, "_____?" Dave was so startled, he didn't
(question)

know what to say. Just as he was about to open his _____,
(body part)

Tasha's big, hairy _____ raced into the room, took
(animal)

one look at Dave, and began to _____. Meanwhile,
(verb)

Tasha's mother, who hadn't heard the doorbell, turned on the radio in the next room and began singing along to _____.
(name of music group)

Now, everyone in the family knew that Tasha's mom had recently won the singing award for most_____ at the local music competition for
(adjective)

people over _____. Just as her mother hit the high note C
(number)

with her _____, Tasha _____
(body part)   (verb)

Dave out the door, into the _____, and away into the night.
(noun)

Standards

4. Determine or clarify the meaning of unknown and multiple-meaning words and phrases by using context clues, analyzing meaningful word parts, and consulting general and specialized reference materials, as appropriate.
5. Demonstrate understanding of figurative language, word relationships, and nuances in word meanings.
6. Acquire and use accurately a range of general academic and domain-specific words and phrases sufficient for reading, writing, speaking, and listening at the college and career readiness level; demonstrate independence in gathering vocabulary knowledge when considering a word or phrase important to comprehension or expression.

EXERCISE 2.10

One of the reasons English has lasted as a distinct language for so many centuries is its users' ability to create easily understandable new words through the combination of already existing root words, suffixes, and prefixes. For examples of the flexibility of the English language to fit all kinds of contexts, just think about the recent terms coined for reporting current events: criticism of *Obamacare*, the *post-9/11* mindset, movies about a *bromance*, and so on. Ask your students to demonstrate their understanding of how American English users build new words by having them create their own. What activity or idea in their own lives needs a new word to describe it? For example, a number of exams in a row might be an *examathon*, or maybe some of your students would enjoy a *footballpalooza*. Table 2.5 provides a list of prefixes and suffixes, which may give them some ideas for new combinations.

Guided Questions for Class Discussion

1. Ask students to share their words with each other, either individually or in small groups. Can the other students understand what the new word means? Why? They should be able to analyze and discuss how they identified individual elements of the word and then combined them together to create a different meaning.
2. Can students use their new words in a sentence? What part of speech are they? Now ask each student to turn the new word into another part of speech. For example, if it's a noun, can they make an adjective or a verb out of it?
3. Ask students to discuss the possibility of their new words becoming part of the American vocabulary. What causes a new word to get adopted for use across the country?

Table 2.5 Commonly Used Prefixes and Suffixes

Prefix	Meaning	Example	Suffix	Meaning	Example
Anti-	Against	Anti-virus	-able, -ible	Capable of, worthy	Dependable
Arch-	Supreme (in a positive or a negative sense)	Arch-enemy	-ant	Quality of, one who	Defiant
Co-	Joint, accompanying	Co-captain	-er, -or	Agent, one who	Actor
Dis-	Opposite of, not	Dis-enchanted	-ful	Of	Graceful
Ex-	Former	Ex-Marine	-ic	Like, made of	Metallic
Post-	After	Post-prom	-less	Without	Careless
Pre-	Before	Pre-register	-let	Small	Starlet
Pro-	For, on the side of	Pro-war	-ship	Quality of, state of	Governorship
Re-	Again	Re-run	-wise	Direction	Clockwise

MEETING STUDENTS WHERE THEY ARE

Once students become aware of code-switching, and their own code-switching practices, they will be able to recognize how important this skill is in American culture as a whole. Every individual, from the President to a child in elementary school, changes his/her language as he/she moves from one rhetorical situation to another. It might be as minor a change as using a different vocabulary or pronunciation, or it might be the more complex shift from informal to formal language use, or even moving from one language to another.

This exercise invites students to develop their own observational and critical thinking skills as they make the change from being passive audience members to critical listeners and analysts of popular culture. It could easily be adapted from a group to an individual exercise and/or from a written assignment to an oral presentation.

Ask students to visit at least one of the following web sites, which contain clips of famous American rappers being interviewed by national media representatives. Next have students find these artists' song lyrics on-line. Students should be able to identify ways in which the language used in the rappers' songs differs from that found in the recorded conversations. We are assuming that these artists are popular enough that students will be immediately familiar with some of their work. You could, however, easily find other artists, representative lyrics, and/or videos for illustrations, if you wish.

For their analysis, ask students to identify as many differences as possible between the language used in the music and the language used in the interview. They could begin, for example, with thinking about rhyme and rhythm, then thinking about the more complicated elements of subject matter, word choice, and tone. And with a little guidance, they should be able to understand why these artists may switch from one language use to another. Why, for example, might rappers speak about illegal activities, such as violence or drug use, in one way in a song but in another way in an interview? Are they being hypocritical? This might lead into a discussion of persona and voice, as well as student reflections on audience and purpose.

Rapper Jay-Z

Compare/contrast the language Jay-Z uses about the topic of the US music industry, when speaking in an interview with Warren Buffet with the language he uses in his song lyrics for "Moment of Clarity" and/or "Renegade": http://video.forbes.com/fvn/forbes400-10/how-the-music-business-changed-me.

Compare/contrast the language rapper Jay-Z uses when speaking about his life in an interview on the weekly radio program "Fresh Air" with the language he uses in any of his song lyrics discussing his past: http://www.npr.org/2010/11/15/131334322/the-fresh-air-interview-jay-z-decoded.

Rapper Eminem

Compare/contrast the language rapper Eminem uses to discuss his state of sobriety in an interview on the weekly radio program "Fresh Air" with the language he uses in any of his earlier songs describing his drug use, such as "Must be the Ganja": http://www.npr.org/templates/story/story.php?storyId=127953120.

Guided Questions for Class Discussion

1. What specific examples of code-switching can your students identify? Ask them to describe what has changed in the speaker's language use from one context to another: vocabulary, pronunciation, tone, type of utterances, etc.
2. Ask your students to consider why the speaker uses particular usages in one setting and something different in another. For example, why are profanities acceptable in song lyrics but not in a TV interview? Has the speaker shifted settings? Changed topic or audience? What has changed about the context that would cause the same person to speak about the same subject using very different language?

LOOKING TO THE FUTURE

In college and the work world, students will encounter many different genres of writing that they will need to learn and use. Learning these genres, of course, entails learning the language usage appropriate to each one in order to code-switch effectively among them.

One common college major and career choice, business, is a discipline that employs diverse written genres. Success at writing these genres depends heavily upon considerations of purpose and audience. For the next exercise, ask students to work in groups as they analyze the examples of a resumé and a business letter given below. Questions to guide students in their analyses appear below. And they may find using Table 2.6 helpful as they compare/contrast these two texts.

Table 2.6 Rubric for *Looking to the Future* Exercise

	Resumé	Business Letter
Purpose		
Intended audience		
Reader expectations of content		
Tone		
Reader expectations of format		
Type of sentences		

Guided Questions for Class Discussion

1. Ask students to discuss for what purposes a resumé might be written. Who is the typical audience for a resumé? What should be foregrounded in a resumé?
2. How familiar are your students with the genre of business letters? Do they know some of the reasons for writing business letters? The tone of a typical business letter? What are the usual expectations that a reader has of a business letter? For instance, what kind of salutation is typically used? What is most often stated in the first paragraph? What kind of closing is often used?

Resumé Example:

John Jones
888-888-8888
1111 S. Broad St., Ogden, Utah 77777
jjones1@xyz.net

Objective
To gain an entry-level sales position with a national business-development company

Education
University of Michigan
B.S. in Psychology (2012)

Awards:
    Dean's List in 2010 and 2011
    Student Achievement Scholarship in 2011

Volunteerism:
    Red Cross Emergency Team 2010-2012

Activities:
    Campus Radio Station DJ (WWWX)
    Psychology Club

Professional Experience
- Sales Clerk, Bright's Bookstore   May, 2010–Aug, 2011
  Ogden, UT
  Responsibilities: Stock shelves, assist customers in finding appropriate books, act as cashier, answer phone queries, assist in monthly inventory

- Server, International House of Pancakes   May, 2009–Aug, 2009
  Ogden, UT
  Responsibilities: Stock service station and prepare tables for opening, interact with customers by taking orders and serving food correctly, follow guidelines for special diets, input orders on computer system, and prepare bills

- Server, Randolph's Road House   May, 2007–Aug, 2007
  Ogden, UT   May, 2008–Aug, 2008
  Responsibilities: Interact with customers by taking orders and serving food correctly, follow guidelines for special diets, stock service station, input orders on computer system, prepare bills, and assist as needed in closing

Business Letter Example:

555 Green St.
Reno, NV 87605
May 27, 2012

Jane Smith
J. Smith Pre-Owned Vehicles
543 E. Main St.
Reno, NV 87602

Dear Mrs. Smith:

On March 29th of this year, I bought a 2009 Chevrolet Impala from your dealership. I was pleased with the car until about two weeks later when the engine began to make a funny sound. I brought the car in to be checked by my mechanic, but he couldn't find anything wrong. A week later, the alternator died. I immediately called the salesman who sold me the car, and he told me to contact the Service Department. I did, and was told that I would have to have the car towed at my own expense to your service center where they would replace the alternator for free. I had the car towed and the new alternator was installed.

Today I am writing to request reimbursement for the cost of towing the car. Since the car was still under our state's "lemon law," it was your company's duty to fix any problems with the car, which you did. But, I feel that any money I am out to get the repairs made, including towing, should be covered by you. When I suggested this to your Service Dept. personnel, they simply replied that it was J. Smith's policy not to cover towing fees. This seems very unfair to me. Please reimburse me $75 for the cost of the towing. Thank you.

Sincerely,

John Jones

SUGGESTED FURTHER READING

Language and Identity

Lakoff, G. and Johnson, M. (2003). *Metaphors we live by* (2nd ed.). Chicago: University of Chicago Press. In this classic exploration of language and the mind, the authors examine how language, and metaphors in particular, help us to understand ourselves and our world.

Pinker, S. (2008). *The stuff of thought: Language as a window into human nature*. New York: Penguin. In this highly accessible book about human language, Pinker argues that by examining our words, we can find out who we are.

Code-switching

Denham, K. and Lobeck, A. (Eds.) (2010). *Linguistics at school: Language awareness in primary and secondary education*. New York: Cambridge University Press. This collection of essays reveals the numerous ways in which the fields of linguistics and education overlap by focusing on three specific arenas: the institution of education, the language arts program, and the language arts classroom.

Turner, K. H. (2009). Flipping the switch: Code-switching from text speak to standard English, *English Journal 98*(5), 60–65. Turner examines the value of using the language of texting as a way of making her students more aware of the need to match language use to context. She sets her discussion in the context of Wheeler and Swords' work, and includes a thorough description, including a handout, of the exercise she used in her own class.

Wheeler, R. S. and Swords, R. (2006). *Code-switching: Teaching standard English in urban classrooms*. Urbana, IL: NCTE. Wheeler and Swords, the recognized authorities on the topic of code-switching in education, explore the topic from several different perspectives in this text. In addition to suggestions for teaching children about language patterns, they also examine the problems teachers face in multidialectal classrooms and the harm teachers can cause when they are unaware of their judgments on dialect use.

Words and Word Relationships

Goddard, C. (1998). *Semantic analysis*. Oxford: Oxford University Press. In this work, the author surveys theories of linguistic meaning, including concepts on word relationships and sequencing.

Marconi, D. (1997). *Lexical competence*. Cambridge, MA: MIT Press. A professor of philosophy of language, Marconi explores humans' lexical competence, their ability to infer and derive meaning from words.

Chapter 3

Speaking and Listening

No one should be surprised, given our highly verbal society, that the CCSS include speaking and listening outcomes. But rather than being just a slight addition to the traditional "reading and writing and 'rithmetic" that many expect to be the foundation for academic studies, the CCSS instead include Speaking and Listening as a separate category, equally important to the outcomes for the Reading, Writing, and Language categories. This equal emphasis supports the notion that speaking and listening skills are an essential component of the language arts discipline, and that they are integrally related to the skills of reading and writing. The NCTE definition of literacy (2008) points out that in contemporary society, unlike in the past, reading and writing skills do not exist in isolation:

> *Literacy has always been a collection of cultural and communicative practices shared among members of particular groups. As society and technology change, so does literacy. Because*

technology has increased the intensity and complexity of literate environments, the twenty-first century demands that a literate person possess a wide range of abilities and competencies.

The NCTE statement ends by describing representative 21st-century work-place tasks, illustrating the ways in which different language arts skills, including speaking and listening, are combined. For example, the business world demands workers who can build "relationships with others to pose and solve problems collaboratively and cross-culturally," and who can design and share "information for global communities to meet a variety of purposes." So we must recognize that, to be literate today and successful both in college and the workforce, our students must be effective in the skills of speaking and listening.

LANGUAGE PROCESSING

Being a good listener is essential in today's world. In school, students may spend as much as 50% of their time listening (Strother, 1987; Wolvin and Coakley, 1988). And in the work-place, employees typically listen 3–4 times more than they speak (Grognet and Van Duzer, 2000), while top executives spend twice as much time listening as other employees (Kotter, 1982).

Note that these kinds of listening contexts require an intellectual thought process in which persons must process and then respond to information being given. The notion of *processing* language arises from psycholinguistic research on cognitive thinking: linguists suggest that processing mechanisms in the brain, specific neural circuits, pick up information from hearing language, quickly process it, and then activate meaning. (See Figure 3.1.)

Figure 3.1 How the Brain Converts Sounds to Meaning

Thus the brain may function much like the way a computer processor functions, working along pathways that are mandatory and automatic, arriving in milliseconds at an "answer" (Fodor, 1983; Garrett, 1988). Drawing upon this linguistic research, other scholars in organizational and behavioral sciences (Purdy and Borisoff, 1996; Brownell, 2009) have hypothesized the many different actions functioning within the language processing system. Among these, listeners must determine a reason for listening (why should they bother?); take "raw" speech, store it in their short-term memories, and attempt to understand its meaning; recall background information to help interpret the message; check that they've understood the meaning; and, finally, may choose to store part of the message in their long-term memories. Although persons perform many of these actions subconsciously, their abilities to do so effectively can be practiced and improved upon, and so schools can truly help students become better active listeners and communicators. And development of these skills is critical to their future success, as recognized by the authors of the CCSS who write, "whatever their intended major or profession, high school graduates will depend heavily on their ability to listen attentively to others so that they are able to build on others' meritorious ideas while expressing their own clearly and persuasively" (Note, Speaking and Listening Standards, p. 48).

MASTERING GROUP COMMUNICATION

Beginning in the elementary years, teachers train their students to "pay attention," that is, to listen to what is going on in class, especially to what the teacher is saying, reading, announcing, etc. In the high school years, a different type of listening training may take place as teachers prepare students for college and the workforce. In fact, the very first Anchor Standard for Speaking and Listening recognizes this different focus, stating that graduating high school students should be able to *prepare for and participate effectively in a range of conversations and collaborations with diverse partners, building on others' ideas and expressing their own clearly and persuasively*.

Once students get into college and the workforce, they will be required to work in a variety of ways and settings, from solving problems on a small team, to finding out information in a study group, to brainstorming ideas with a coworker, and so on. Each work procedure requires individuals to be able to guide themselves, as well as others, toward completing a task, and so it becomes critical that students know how to engage in productive discussion and collaboration. Identifying the kind of language behaviors required in collaboration can help students to achieve this goal.

Linguists have suggested that language fulfills two principle functions: it expresses content, and it expresses social relations and personal attitudes. Students probably are more familiar with the second function since their worlds revolve around their peer groups and friends, communities in which language can be casual, intimate, and personal. Brown and Yule (1983) have termed this kind of language "interactional," because its primary function is to establish and maintain social relationships, for instance, conversations to establish roles, e.g. between parents and children, or workers on a job; or to reinforce peer relationships, e.g. between friends or acquaintances. (See Figure 3.2.) Different from interactional discourse is "transactional" discourse, which expresses content. Most group work, whether in a classroom or a business setting, is transactional: any time group members work together and use skills, such as asking questions, explaining, repeating, summarizing, and so on, they

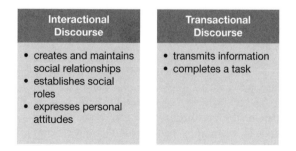

Figure 3.2 Two Types of Discourse Present in the Classroom

are involved in transactional discourse. The Anchor Standards acknowledge the importance of having transactional discourse skills when they specifically identify the tasks students should be able to complete in any sort of group activity: "informal consensus, voting on key issues, and presentation of alternate views" (p. 50). To help students understand the communication skills needed for different kinds of discourse contexts, the following exercise asks them to compare a personal conversation with friends (interactional discourse) to a group work assignment (transactional discourse).

Standard

1. Prepare for and participate effectively in a range of conversations and collaborations with diverse partners, building on others' ideas and expressing their own clearly and persuasively.

EXERCISE 3.1

This exercise asks students to consider the different kinds of communication skills needed in personal conversation and group work, focusing on the common discourse techniques listed below. Students should participate in all three parts of the exercise so that they can compare different discourse contexts and their conventions.

Common Communication Skills
Listening
Asking questions
Explaining
Describing
Repeating
Summarizing
Getting attention
Directing attention
Taking turns
Revising
Repairing error/miscommunication
Encouragement

Part 1: Have each student in the class imagine talking with a friend about what seems to be an excessive amount of homework. Give them 5 minutes to do some thinking about the nature of that conversation and to make notes about their ideas. They may like to consider the following questions as they gather their thoughts: When and where might such a conversation take place? What might be the purpose of such a conversation? Which communication skills from the list above might each person employ in this type of conversation?

Part 2: Divide your students into groups of no more than 4 students each and give each group 10 minutes to define the line between an acceptable and an unacceptable amount of homework. Students may come up with several definitions. After they've discussed the topic, ask each group to analyze their discussion process, with each student making notes of their peers' comments. Students may like to consider the following questions as they analyze their group discussions: Which communication skills from the list above did members in your group employ? Did your group reach a consensus (a general agreement) on the definition of acceptable and unacceptable amounts of homework? Were some persons in the group more listeners than talkers, and, conversely, more talkers than listeners? If so, what was the result of this? How quickly was your group able to produce a definition? What were some factors that affected the length of time needed?

Part 3: In a full-class discussion, ask students to compare/contrast these two different types of communication, with the ultimate goal of making suggestions for improving the process and outcomes of each.

Guided Questions for Class Discussion

1. Can students add any discourse techniques to this list that they use either in a group or in conversing with a friend?
2. What techniques were shared by both group and personal communications? Why?
3. What techniques were unique to either the group or the personal communication? Why? What's different between these two types of discourse?
4. How do the techniques identified as appropriate for only one or the other type of discourse improve that type of communication?

EXERCISE 3.2

This exercise helps students to practice transactional discourse by undertaking a common group task—problem-solving—but the emphasis of the activity lies on analyzing the group's process of communication rather than achieving a particular solution.

1. Divide the class up into several groups of 5–6 students each, and explain that each group should work to solve the assigned problem by reaching a consensus among all members of the group. Members should only support a solution that they can truly accept to some degree; in other words, they should not agree with something just to complete the task. In addition, there should be no designated leader of the group: all must work together to understand, discuss, and eventually come up with a solution. As students work through this exercise, they should be aware of their group dynamic—the questions below will help them to critique their process.
2. Give a handout describing the problem to each group member. Any problem relevant to your students would be appropriate for this exercise, such as a current issue at the high school or in the surrounding community. Figure 3.3 illustrates a handout you could use.

In the last two weeks, 6–7 juniors and seniors going off campus at lunchtime have created disturbances in the neighboring businesses, including engaging in activities such as loitering, suspected shoplifting from a local drug store and a grocery (no perpetrators caught), a fist fight in front of a 7-11, breaking bottles in the street, and interfering with pedestrian traffic. The businesses have banded together and demanded that the high school principal and staff do something about this. It is a longstanding practice of the high school that juniors and seniors have been allowed to go off campus for lunch.

Your group's task is to find an appropriate solution to this problem, a solution that will recognize all constituents of the issue and that can be implemented at low cost and expected full compliance.

Figure 3.3 Sample Handout for Exercise 3.2

3. Once the problem has been read and understood, give students 10 minutes to discuss the issue and come up with a solution.
4. After 10 minutes of discussion, ask students to free write for 10 minutes, assessing and evaluating the discussion in their group, using the questions below as a guide.
5. Bring the groups back into full class discussion and ask each group about the solutions they came up with. Finally, having them use their written notes as guides, ask them to offer advice that would allow future group discussion activities to be more successful.

Guided Questions for Individual Student Analysis of Group Discussion

1. Did every member of your group speak up and participate in the discussion?
2. Did some participate more than others? Why do you think they did?
3. Were all ideas respected and considered by the group?
4. Did anyone's ideas fail to be discussed? If yes, why so?
5. Were members of the group willing to listen to others? What in their comments and body language indicated this?
6. Was the full 10 minutes wisely used? In other words, was the group working toward a solution the whole time?
7. Were some solutions discussed and accepted, but then later rejected? Why?
8. Was it difficult for your group to reach consensus? Why or why not?
9. Which of the discourse strategies from the list above did the group use?

Standard

4. Present information, findings, and supporting evidence such that listeners can follow the line of reasoning and the organization, development, and style are appropriate to task, purpose, and audience.

Exercise Extension

Instead of having students discuss as a class what they learned about successful group discussion techniques (Step #5 above), ask students in their groups to prepare a short presentation to be delivered to the rest of the class. The presentation should briefly critique their own discussion and then should offer 2–3 suggestions for successfully conducting group work.

EVALUATING DIVERSE MEDIA

Recognizing the many and varied ways in which information is delivered today, the Anchor Standards for Speaking and Listening state that students should be able to analyze and evaluate diverse modalities under the broad categories of oral and visual communication. Each medium has its own conventions and typically produces distinct effects on its audience. To be savvy consumers of information in the world today, students must have knowledge of the ways in which diverse media convey their messages.

Although students easily recognize the basic differences between delivering information orally and visually, they may not have considered the distinctive rhetorical effects of each medium. For instance, most oral communication involves much more than just words: the most effective speakers will employ a range of tones, registers, gestures, and other elements to create the most impact on their listeners. All of these elements add meaning to the actual words themselves. While written texts may describe these elements, the effects are usually not as strong as when listeners can hear for themselves. If you point out to your students the difference between reading a novel and then seeing it visually enacted on a movie screen, they'll understand how different media create different effects. The following exercise is intended to help your students understand these differences by examining one text rendered in oral, written, and visual formats.

Standards

2. Integrate and evaluate information presented in diverse media and formats, including visually, quantitatively, and orally.
3. Evaluate a speaker's point of view, reasoning, and use of evidence and rhetoric.

EXERCISE 3.3

Ask students to go the *American Rhetoric* web site (http://www.americanrhetoric. com/speeches/jasonlezakolympicfreestylerelayvictory.htm) where they will find both a transcript and video from NBC network television coverage of the Olympic 4 ×100 freestyle relay race held in Beijing in 2008.

Have them read through the written transcript and think about its effects on its reading audience. Next, tell students to view the video and listen to the television coverage of the race. Using the guided questions below, ask students to compare the two forms of communication. Table 3.1 provides a guide for their analysis. (Note that any part of this exercise leading up to class discussion can be assigned as homework.)

Table 3.1 Rubric for Exercise 3.3

	TV Video	*Written Transcript*
How is emotion shown? How is suspense created? What are the effects on the audience?		

Guided Questions for Class Discussion

1. Ask students how emotion is shown in the written version of the reporting of the swim relay. How is it shown in the spoken version? Which version do they believe has a stronger effect on the audience? Why?
2. Have students consider how the announcers create suspense in their reporting (both written and oral). What would be lost in the reporting if there were no suspense created?
3. Ask students to describe the effect of Hicks' essentially calling the race's conclusion before it is finished (see third comment). How might the audience feel at this moment and then after it's all over?

Exercise Extension

Exercise 3.3 above asks students to go to the *American Rhetoric* web site where they will be able to both hear the announcers and see a video of the actual race. Ask students to imagine if the web site contained only the audio portion of the broadcast, thus allowing the audience to hear, but not see, the race. Then ask them to consider, and/or briefly jot down their ideas, about how one medium alone affects the audience's experience. Questions to consider: How does having only the audio change the emotional tenor of the broadcast? What aspects of the race become less or more emphasized in the audio alone? Can they think of any other discourse contexts in which only the audio, or perhaps only the visual, is employed? What might be the benefits or drawbacks of this kind of transmission?

ANALYZING SPEECHES

Your students will encounter situations in school and beyond that ask them both to listen to and to deliver oral presentations. It's our guess that most teachers offer students guidelines to making successful speeches, but that they give fewer resources to help students practice their listening capabilities. But, as we note above, working on listening skills is an important component of communication education: we receive much information via oral communication and so it's crucial that we teach our students how to listen, process, and respond to what they hear.

One of the most common forms of public oral communication is the speech. Whether delivered in a church, senate, beauty pageant, campaign, or other arena, a speech is persuasive in nature: the speaker is always trying to convince the listeners of something. Ever since Aristotle first identified the three principle means of persuasion, successful orators have endeavored to employ these approaches in their speeches in order to persuade listeners of their arguments: (1) persuasion by presenting a credible public persona; (2) persuasion by using arguments based upon logic and reason; and (3) persuasion by appealing to the emotions of listeners. (See Figure 3.4.) Notice that the success of the speaker in using these approaches rests upon the audience's reactions: Do they find the speaker credible? Do they find the argument logical, reasonable, and therefore truthful? Has the speaker tapped their emotions in authentic and relevant ways? Audience members thus become active participants in the process: they are listening, and they are actively engaged by the speaker. This is why it's so important that listeners understand the message that the speech contains, as well as the methods employed by the speaker to convince them of that message. Students may want to know why they should consider the latter, the methods employed. The following exercise helps to explain why knowledge of the rhetoric of speech-making is important.

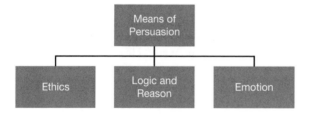

Figure 3.4 Aristotle's Persuasive Appeals

Standard

3. Evaluate a speaker's point of view, reasoning, and use of evidence and rhetoric.

EXERCISE 3.4

Have students read the following short speeches and then as a class discuss each speech's effects on its audience, as well as its overall effectiveness. Use the guided questions to help ground your discussion. Table 3.2 provides a guide for your students' analysis.

Table 3.2 Rubric for Exercise 3.4

	Speech #1	Speech #2	Speech #3
Purpose			
Intended audience			
Audience's connection to topic			
Persuasive appeal			

Speech #1: "Why I'm the Most Qualified Candidate for Student Council President"
Speaker: Junior in high school
Audience: whole student body in an assembly

Hi,
I'd like you to vote for me because I'm the best person for the job. My older brother was Student Council President and people tell me that I'm like him, so I'm sure I'd be good at it. I also have my brother's wicked sense of humor, which might be good to have in meetings. I've always liked to be on committees and stuff, helping to organize events. If you vote for me, you won't be sorry—I'll bring a lot of change to Eastern High School and change is always good.

Speech #2: "Plea to Install Video Cameras in Downtown Intersections"
Speaker: City resident at a City Council meeting
Audience: City Council

Hello, Concerned City Council Members:
When each one of you took the oath of office, you promised to protect the lives of our citizens. I am sorry to say that you have failed miserably at the job. There have been several traffic accidents and robberies in our streets in the last year, and I'm afraid it's just getting worse. Just last week, my daughter's book bag was stolen by a group of teenagers, and she lost her cell phone and some money. She cried for two days and wouldn't go out of the house because she was so scared and upset. There's a silver lining behind these dark clouds, however. You have one last chance to show that you are sincere in wanting to help others: by voting to buy video cameras to be placed in our major intersections, you will demonstrate to our residents that you care. Please think of the lives saved and vote for life, not death!

Speech #3: Speech about placing the topic, "The Effects of Video Gaming," on the program for the annual convention of the National Association of Parenting
Speaker: Parent and member of organization
Audience: National Association of Parenting conference program committee

Fellow Parents and Members of NAP,
I come before you to request that you add a panel on "The Effects of Video Gaming" to your annual conference program. I believe that it would be a topic of interest to many of the conference-goers and that the panel would be well-attended. The effects of video gaming are of serious concern to many parents. Just the other day, I read in the paper that a doctor at our hospital said that gaming might be bad for children. And the senior minister in my church also voiced his concern. It's a timely topic and I hope that you can include it. Thank you.

Guided Questions for Class Discussion

1. For each speech above, ask students to consider the speaker's purposes: What argument is he/she making? What is he/she trying to persuade the audience of?
2. Have students consider what the intended audience for each speech might already know and might like to know further about the topic. What are their expectations of the speaker, and what is their interest in the topic?
3. Ask students to examine the points that each speaker has used to further his argument. How effective is each? Does it relate to the argument? Would a listener be convinced by it?
4. Review with students the three rhetorical approaches mentioned above for appealing to an audience. Ask students to identify the ways that each speaker has used. Does the way(s) the speaker has chosen seem to be appropriate to the argument? In other words, is it the most effective approach? Why or why not?
5. Have students think about what might be missing from each of these speeches. What else did the speaker need to include?

Now that your students have had a chance to consider some of the elements of speech-making, they are ready to do a more in-depth analysis of a noted speech. You know that as part of their cultural knowledge, students must be familiar with many of the important speeches that have helped to define our country. All school standards, including the CCSS, recognize that speeches form part of the corpus of informational texts that our students should be exposed to. The following exercise asks students to examine a speech that they probably know well: Abraham Lincoln's "Gettysburg Address." Different from previous lessons on Lincoln's work, however, which may have focused on its content alone, this exercise asks students to explore both its substance and its rhetorical style.

EXERCISE 3.5

Have students read the following text of "The Gettysburg Address." Ask them to answer the questions following the passage as they examine the text rhetorically, either as a class or in small groups.

Background on the speech: President Lincoln delivered this address on November 19, 1863 at the dedication of the Gettysburg National Cemetery in Pennsylvania. The cemetery was created to memorialize the over 3,500 Union soldiers who had died four months before, during the Battle of Gettysburg. The Union Army won the Battle of Gettysburg, but, at the time of the cemetery dedication, the outcome of the war was far from certain.

The Gettysburg Address
Four score and seven years ago our fathers brought forth on this continent, a new nation, conceived in Liberty, and dedicated to the proposition that all men are created equal.

Now we are engaged in a great civil war, testing whether that nation, or any nation so conceived and so dedicated, can long endure. We are met on a great battlefield of that war. We have come to dedicate a portion of that field, as a final resting place for those who here gave their lives that that nation might live. It is altogether fitting and proper that we should do this.

But, in a larger sense, we cannot dedicate—we cannot consecrate—we cannot hallow—this ground. The brave men, living and dead, who struggled here, have consecrated it, far above our poor power to add or detract. The world will little note, nor long remember what we say here, but it can never forget what they did here. It is for us the living, rather, to be dedicated here to the unfinished work which they who fought here have thus far so nobly advanced. It is rather for us to be here dedicated to the great task remaining before us—that from these honored dead we take increased devotion to that cause for which they gave the last full measure of devotion—that we here highly resolve that these dead shall not have died in vain—that this nation, under God, shall have a new birth of freedom—and that government of the people, by the people, for the people, shall not perish from the earth.

Guided Questions for Class Discussion

1. Ask students how the Address reveals that Lincoln had several purposes for going to Gettysburg and giving this speech.
2. Have students think about who might have been the audience listening to Lincoln's speech. What might have been their expectations for the speech? What did they want to hear?
3. Have students discuss why Lincoln begins the speech with a reference to 1776, and the founding of this country. Why use the phrase "four score and seven years" instead of the more commonly used number, "eighty-seven"?
4. What obligation does Lincoln suggest that his listeners have?
5. Ask students to consider the effect of saying that "the world will little note, nor long remember what we say here." Why does Lincoln say this line?
6. Have students count how many times the word "I" is used in the speech. How many times "we" or "us"? Why has Lincoln chosen to use the latter terms?
7. Lincoln's address is noted for, among other things, its effective use of repetition and parallelism (similarity of structure in a pair or in a series of words, phrases, or sentences): ask students to find words, phrases, and sentence structures that repeat. What is the effect of these repetitions?

Standard

2. Integrate and evaluate information presented in diverse media and formats, including visually, quantitatively, and orally.

Exercise Extension

An exercise that your students might have fun doing is comparing different audio versions of "The Gettysburg Address." Not only will they be able to see the differences between reading a speech and listening to one, but they will also explore the various and varying effects produced by different orators.

In 1863 when Lincoln delivered his speech, amplification and recording were not yet possible, but ever since technology was made available in the late 1800s, "The Gettysburg Address" has often been recorded. The following link takes you to the *American Rhetoric* web site, a compilation of famous American speeches, where you will hear six different versions of the address spoken by six different speakers. The speakers include a classical singer who recorded his version in 1898, a country music superstar, a Hollywood actor, and others: http://www.americanrhetoric. com/speeches/gettysburgaddress.htm.

Have students listen to one or more of the speech versions and compare their deliveries and effects, using the following guidelines and questions. Ask students to write up their comparisons in a 1–2 page analysis to be handed in.

Guided Questions for Class Discussion

1. Choosing 2–3 speeches, compare the use of the following elements found in each: stressing of particular words, pausing, and pace (speed). If you find differences, try to figure out why the speakers might have chosen to speak the lines the way they did: What effect might they have wanted to produce in the listener? What ideas or emotions, apparently, did each speaker feel were important to convey?
2. Just through their speech, these six speakers reveal an array of diverse characteristics, such as age, regional accent, and, perhaps, educational or socio-economic level. Consider each of these characteristics, and discuss how they may produce different effects on the listener for each speech. Does sounding like one is from a particular part of the country, for instance, make one's performance less effective? More effective? Why?
3. In several of the speeches, there is background noise, from the scratchiness of the recording equipment in W. F. Hooley's 1898 version, to the quiet guitar strumming accompanying Johnny Cash's rendition. Another speech has the sound of the audience clapping both before and after the speech. What is the effect of these sounds on the overall performance of the orator? Do the sounds detract from the words? Heighten the importance of the event? Add a corniness to the recording?

Exercise Extension

Students are probably well-aware of the importance of "The Gettysburg Address" for what it says about patriotism, respect, courage, and honor. It is considered a seminal text because of its timeliness in a conflict that threatened to divide and thus change forever the United States of America. Lincoln knew that the Battle of Gettysburg was a turning point in the war, not because the outcome of the war was certain but because it marked a halfway point in the long siege and could galvanize people to commit to the Union side, the side that the Address implies has right and honor on its side.

Students may not be aware that "The Gettysburg Address" has been used during other commemorations in this country. For instance, the Mayor of New York read "The Gettysburg Address" at the first anniversary of the terrorist attacks on September 11, 2001. And veterans of other wars of this country have also used commemorative ceremonies to recite the address. Have students research the uses of "The Gettysburg Address" in contemporary times: When and where has it been used? Have them write up the results of their research and then reflect on what they've found. Why might this speech, which seemingly belongs to a very particular time and place, resonate with people today in very different places?

LANGUAGE STYLE

Adapting Speech

As you know, an individual's educational level, socioeconomic status, age, gender, and so on all shape his/her language use. But these external factors are not the only things influencing usage: people also have the power to shape their language through the choices they make of particular words, sentence structures, tone, etc., in response to specific situations. Everyone has the ability to vary his/her language, adapting it to be appropriate for each discourse context. These variations, referred to as styles or registers, enable language users to convey not only literal meaning with their words, but also a wide range of information, including an acknowledgment of their positions in the hierarchy of social setting and an indication of the social distance between them and a specific audience. For an example, have your students think about a person speaking politely to a superior at work and then going home and whining to a best friend. Choosing to use polite language to a superior indicates respect, both in terms of hierarchy and distance, while whining shows recognition of equal status and personal closeness. It's important for your students to know that making the wrong stylistic choice can have serious repercussions. Continuing the example above, whining to a superior at work may lose someone a job, while being formally polite to a friend may end the friendship. Students must learn that every aspect of language use—word choice, tone, formality, etc.—affects meaning, and thus the appropriateness of the message. Authors of the Speaking and Listening Standards recognize this imperative when they mandate that students must be able to *adapt speech to a variety of contexts and communicative tasks, demonstrating command of formal English when indicated or appropriate* (#6).

Because they're able to adapt their language to fit each purpose and audience, successful adults move through a range of styles over the course of a day, from formal to informal and back again. But students are frequently unaware of subtle language shifts matching language style to social context and of the social implications for inappropriate language use. In fact, research shows that children growing up in poverty not only fail to gain mastery of but may not even understand the formal language styles used in school and in academic testing (Payne, 2008). The research seems to suggest then that schools need to directly teach students about the ties between language style and social context, rather than take such awareness for granted and thereby handicap students who lack this knowledge (Knestrict and Schoensteadt, 2005; Wheeler and Swords, 2006). Because the number of language

Table 3.3 Language Style Varies According to Each Social Situation

Level of Formality:	Casual	Consultative	Formal	Frozen
Example	Chat with friends	Casual business communication, conversation in school	Testing in schools, government publications, public speeches	Shakespeare play, Miranda rights
Social relationship	Friends and insiders	Strangers and near strangers working together in routine ways	Awareness of social hierarchy and personal distance	Art, ritual, and ceremony
Use of names	Nicknames, "I" & "you" personal pronouns	Limited nicknames, use of given name, "I" & "you" personal pronouns	No nicknames, no "I" & "you" personal pronouns, use of title and last name	Honorific plus full name
Density of meaning/quantity of communication	Low density/unlimited quantity	Moderate density/limited quantity	High density/limited quantity	High symbolic density/limited quantity
Vocabulary	Slang, taboo words, limited vocabulary of 400–800 words	Less formal SAE, jargon	SAE vocabulary, precise word choice, no slang or jargon	Archaic and/or SAE
Sentence conventions	Contractions, unrestrained sentence fragments, short sentences	Fewer contractions, restrained sentence fragments	Long sentences, varied sentence structures	Concern for euphony

Source: Adapted from Joos (1961)

styles is infinite without clear boundaries delineating their use, students need to be able to assess each language situation to determine what's appropriate.

A commonly used model for identifying and discussing language styles places language contexts along a continuum, from most informal to most formal. Table 3.3 provides one such model, illustrating just a few of the ways in which both written and oral language styles vary to reflect the needs of each social situation and each user.

Remember that this table focuses on generalities. Although it indicates distinct categories, in real life subtle variations exist, making such clear categories untenable. So students can't simply memorize each social context and apply a particular style that will be appropriate. Instead, analyzing the underlying social context will provide the clues for determining the appropriate style for any context. For instance, because informal speech reflects social familiarity between participants, it is subjective, emotional, spontaneous, and largely ephemeral. So it is marked by elements such as contractions, a repetitious vocabulary, and more casual articulation, such as dropping sounds at the end of words (*going* becomes *goin'*) or reducing consonantal clusters (*tooth* becomes *toof*). Toward the other end of the language spectrum, in a formal language style, any communication would be impersonal and precise in all elements, including pronunciation. While spontaneous conversation always uses an informal style, the most formal uses of American English appear in a written form.

Standard

6. Adapt speech to a variety of contexts and communicative tasks, demonstrating command of formal English when indicated or appropriate.

EXERCISE 3.6

Thinking about the range of stylistic choices possible can be overwhelming for inexperienced students. Perhaps showing them how much they already know will provide a helpful way to begin such a conversation. Show the class Table 3.3, or even just a section of it, and ask them to provide some examples of appropriate speech for a few of the contexts. They will know, for example, that a wedding ceremony uses very different language from a mother talking to her baby. Getting them to identify and analyze differences in language in various contexts will help them begin to think about ways to adapt their own language.

EXERCISE 3.7

The following exercise, in two parts, asks students to think about language use in terms of formality, a perspective they're probably unused to considering. Divide the class into small groups of 3–4 students. Tell them to imagine that they're visiting three different kinds of restaurants, ranging from an informal fast food burger joint to a casual family-style restaurant, to a formal 5-star restaurant.

Part 1: Ask the students to use their own experiences, as well as what they've observed on TV and/or film, to describe the language use they might encounter when entering each restaurant. The following questions will help them think about the details: Which employee is the first to speak to them? What is said to them? How do they answer? What tone does the encounter have? How is the menu presented? What does it contain? What elements of language are present in one setting but absent in another? Table 3.4 provides a guide for their analysis.

After the students have compared/contrasted the beginning of these dining

Table 3.4 Rubric for Exercise 3.7

	Fast Food Restaurant	Family-Style Restaurant	5-Star Restaurant
Which employee speaks first?			
Language spoken by employee			
Diner's answer			
Tone of encounter			
Presentation of menu			

experiences, lead the class in an analysis of their observations by asking them to think about social hierarchy and distance: Which dining experience makes the customer feel the most dominant? The least? And why? Which dining experience makes the customer feel the closest to the employee in terms of feeling that the employee cares or that the employee is genuinely interested in helping? And why?

Your students may discover that their expectations are overturned as a result of this discussion. They might expect fast food workers to use the most friendly and personal language because the setting is informal, while in reality these workers are probably the most likely to use a rigid script in order to move the customers through as quickly as possible. Script rigidity frequently makes the customer feel subordinate, even insignificant in response, and thereby risks his complete disassociation, which might mean he/she will never return. And the formal dining experience is the most likely to create as respectful a relationship as possible, making the customer feel dominant over all the employees, possibly a positive outcome, yet some customers may be turned off by this obviously contrived relationship.

Part 2: Ask students, either individually or in small groups, to rank each group of words below from the least formal for the burger joint, to the most formal for the 5-star restaurant, by indicating which term would appear on which menu. The students should be able to explain their reasoning as they think about the relationships between language use and intended audience, including social distance and social hierarchy.

1. raspberry sauce, raspberry coulis, raspberry topping
2. chicken fillets, chicken strips, chicken fingers

3. ice cream, gelato, Blizzard
4. pancake, crepe, flapjack
5. moo juice, milk, leche
6. baked apple pie, tarte aux pommes, apple pastry

EXERCISE 3.8

This exercise asks students to deepen their analysis of language style through a comparison of different types of messages centering on the same topic. Scenarios 1 and 2 illustrate communications about the Health Insurance Portability and Accountability Act (HIPAA), while scenarios 3 and 4 illustrate communications about applying for a job. Students will apply their rhetorical analysis skills to different social situations in order to understand why a particular language style is appropriate. Students may find the chart about language contexts and formality (see Table 3.3) helpful as they begin their analysis. Ask students to read through these communications before working to answer the guided questions at the end.

1. Publication by the Office for Civil Rights, U.S. Department of Health and Human Services. Selection from HIPAA (Health Insurance Portability and Accountability Act) Administrative Simplification: Regulation Text Statute and Rules: Subpart A—General Provisions, §164.105 Organizational requirements:
   (E) If a person performs duties for both the health care component in the capacity of a member of the workforce of such component and for another component of the entity in the same capacity with respect to that component, such workforce member must not use or disclose protected health information created or received in the course of or incident to the member's work for the health care component in a way prohibited by subpart E of this part.
2. Conversation in a pharmacy at the prescription pick-up window:
   Pharmacy tech: "Ma'am, please step back behind that yellow line. We're trying to keep each customer's information private."
3. Email from John Jones to a potential employer:
   Dear Mr. Smith: Please consider my application for the position of Assistant Manager of Sporting Goods that you are currently advertising on the Sears' web site. As you can see from the attached resumé, I have several years of experience in retail sales, and am excited about the possibility of working for a national chain like Sears. If you have any questions or would like to schedule a meeting, please let me know.
   Sincerely, John Jones
4. Phone call to a friend:
   "Hey, man, just applied for that job at Sears. You still like working there?"

Guided Questions for Class Discussion

1. Ask students to consider the social distance and hierarchy between the sender and audience of each message above to determine whether the message is

formal or informal. Then have them consider all four messages on a continuum. Are the formal ones equally formal, or is one more formal than the other? Are the informal ones equally informal, or is one more informal than the other?

2. Ask students which aspects of a social situation and sender/audience seem to determine the level of formality needed.

3. Have students identify the elements in each message that indicate whether it is formal or informal.

Boundaries

Language style also reveals the relationship between an individual and a particular community, that is, whether a person is an insider or an outsider in a certain group. Jargon, for example, is a specialized language style tied to a particular group of people, such as those in the same profession or interested in the same hobby. Jargon expresses the unique concepts and practices of a specific language community and so meets its direct needs. A student who becomes a lawyer, for instance, will use legal jargon in the courtroom or when writing a brief, but will not use it at home with his/her family. Newcomers to a professional community are expected to learn the jargon and use it appropriately. Otherwise they'll never become true members of the community.

But sometimes speakers want to mark their membership in a stigmatized group and so choose to use language of that group, whether accepted by a larger audience or not. This happens all the time in the classroom, such as when students choose to make their friends laugh by using a vulgarity, even though they know the teacher will respond in a negative way. In this situation the students are rebelling against the larger community's representative (the teacher) because they personally value their friends more than the teacher. They would rather be an insider with their community of friends than be seen as an insider with the teacher, or, put another way, the esteem of friends may be worth more than the potential problem of negative consequences.

Slang, another language style that teenagers in particular value, also marks community members, but slang communities are quite different from jargon ones. Slang tends to be spoken, is always informal, and changes rapidly. Many American English speakers incorrectly think that all informal language is slang. But even though all slang is informal, all informal language is not slang. Some American English users view slang as an incorrect style, inferior to SAE, but, in reality, slang is just nonstandardized language. It is inventive, relying heavily on newly coined words and using existing words in new ways. Because it tends to be anti-authoritarian, vulgar-strewn, and nonstandard, slang helps bond community members together. One can't be a member of the "cool clique" without knowing the appropriate slang, so insiders and outsiders are immediately obvious once they open their mouths. Although students may not have a hard time adapting their language to that of a community that uses slang and therefore becoming insiders, they may be less capable of switching registers in other language communities, and so risk remaining as outsiders. The repercussions of being outsiders can be serious: lack of code-switching capabilities can deny one a job, a career, a relationship, or another negative consequence. This is why students need to choose among language styles and registers appropriately. The following exercises will help students think about matching language usage to a particular community and so aid them in beginning to make appropriate choices in their own language use.

EXERCISE 3.9

The following scenarios illustrate the ways that language use identifies insiders and outsiders of specific language communities. In each one, a speaker is using a language that marks him/her as being an outsider in that particular situation.

1. Meeting parents of one's date:
    "Yo, man. Bangin' car, dude!"
2. Interviewing for a technical computer programming job:
    Interviewer: "Explain how you would troubleshoot a problem with a software program loading onto a client's computer."
    Interviewee: "First I'd open the computer, and then I'd push the 'on' button and wait for the computer to finish starting up. Once it was all done, I would click on the image for that particular program and watch to see what happened . . . ."
3. Attending a business meeting to compare/contrast January's income reports from the stores in Wisconsin, California, and Ohio:
    "I used to have an aunt who lived in Ohio. I really disliked visiting her because she never let us play in her backyard. My cousins and I always had to sit in the living room with the grown-ups—very boring!"
4. Sending a text message to a friend:
    "Please be sure to let me know whether or not you want to come with me this evening so that I can purchase the tickets in time."

Guided Questions for Class Discussion

1. Ask students to identify the dominant language community in each situation. How did they know? What language conventions would the people in this community expect to be used?
2. Ask students to explain why each speaker's language is inappropriate for the particular scenario. In what situation would it be appropriate?
3. Have students consider the type of responses each speaker in the above scenarios might receive.
4. How could a speaker unfamiliar with the specific individuals in each scenario determine the language conventions that would be appropriate? Can the students make any generalizations matching language use to community? For instance, does an audience's age impact language use? Education? Experience?

LANGUAGE CHANGE

Anchor Standard #6 for Speaking and Listening directly acknowledges the awareness of language variation that every successful individual needs to have in order to move between personal, academic, and professional language communities: *adapt speech to a variety of contexts and communicative tasks*. But for students to truly be skilled in language usage, they need to expect that language changes over time. The language that they use and study in school as teenagers is not the same language they'll be using as they approach retirement. So any discussion about the ways in which language reflects social relationships also must include an acknowledgment of language change.

Human society constantly changes, and its language changes as well, adding words for new inventions, for instance, and losing words for items no longer in use. Over time, some slang and jargon may spread in use and enter the SAE lexicon. Words such as *bogus* and *mob* were once used only in slang, while computer jargon entered mainstream American English when computers did. Think about how widely understood terms like *desktop*, *Bluetooth*, and *video card* are today, even though they first appeared in a limited context. Even though lexical changes like these occur within a few years, pronunciation changes take place at a slower rate, over decades of time.

Without getting into technical phonological details, students can easily perceive some changes in pronunciation that have taken place over time. They undoubtedly know some of the differences between the way British English and American English are pronounced. And they also are probably aware of how different the language of Shakespeare's time is from that of their own, but they may not know that pronunciation is always shifting; change is not exclusively limited to the past. For example, the 20th century saw the development of the low-back merger (named because it merges two vowel sounds that are pronounced in the lower back of the throat) which has been spreading from Northeastern parts of the United States into the West. In this merger, the sound of the vowel *o* in *cot, box, lot, Don*, and the sound of the diphthong *au/ou/aw* in *caught, fought, bought, dawn* become the same rather than having distinctly different pronunciations. (See Table 3.5.) Although this merger is dominant only in specific sections of the country, linguists speculate that in a few generations, the standard pronunciation for these words across the United States will be the single vowel sound produced by the merger.

All aspects of language—lexicon, pronunciation, usage—change over time, each at a different rate of speed because they're influenced by different factors. And all of these changes come about because of changes in the community that uses the language.

Table 3.5 The Low-Back Merger Results in a Single Vowel Sound

Distinct and Separate Vowel Sounds		Now Pronounced the Same
The Vowel *o*	The Diphthong *au/ou/aw*	
Cot	Caught	Caught
Box	Bought	Bought
Stock	Stalk	Stalk
Don	Dawn	Dawn

EXERCISE 3.10

This exercise asks students to compare/contrast the language used in two TV family sitcoms separated by at least 20 years, in order to identify for themselves some of the ways in which language use has been shifting. The exercise describes a homework assignment, culminating in a short, written essay, but it could easily be adapted to a classroom discussion exercise, using just short clips of the shows.

Ask students to visit Hulu.com and choose two TV family sitcoms, one from the 1980s or earlier (*Alf*, *The Dick Van Dyke Show*, *Bewitched*, etc.) and one of a show produced after 2000 (*Suburgatory*, *How I Met Your Mother*, *8 Simple Rules*, etc.). They should watch each show, taking careful notes about specific uses of language style that they notice: tone, names/titles, politeness, slang, jargon, word choice, sentence structure, etc. They may need to watch each show more than once. Then ask them to write a comparison/contrast essay analyzing the language use in the two shows they chose, explaining whether or not they think American English usage has changed in this relatively short period of time. Table 3.6 will help your students complete their analysis.

Table 3.6 Rubric for Exercise 3.10

	TV Show #1	*TV Show #2*
Naming (use of nicknames, full names, titles, vulgarisms, etc.)		
Politeness (please, thank you, sorry, after you, etc.)		
Level of formality		
References to adult topics (sex, drugs, alcohol, etc.)		
Vocabulary (slang, new words, etc.)		
Sentences (length, complete or fragment)		

MEETING STUDENTS WHERE THEY ARE

When discourse conventions aren't followed, it can be jarring both to the participants in the situation and to those listening in. Greeting a boss with a "Whassup, man?" would raise an eyebrow, as would using SAE in a conversation among friends. Award ceremonies are places where scripts are frequently jettisoned by those involved: over the years, award winners have made political speeches (give gays the right to marry), denounced persons or actions (condemnation of the President, war, Osama Bin Laden), or simply announced their dislike of the winner. Perhaps your students will remember an example of this last kind of comment made by Kanye West at the Grammy Music Awards a few years ago. Have students go to the following web site to view a video of this particular Grammy Awards show. After they've watched it, discuss with them how Kanye departed from the conventions for this kind of event: http://www.youtube.com/watch?v=1z8gCZ7zpsQ.

Guided Questions for Class Discussion

1. Ask students what the typical script for award shows is. What is the expected sequence of events and what is the content of the speeches?
2. Why do audiences tune in and what do they expect to see and hear?
3. Have students identify how West "broke the rules" of the script.
4. What was the audience's reaction? How do you think they felt about West's appearance on stage? Ask your students what their reactions are.
5. Have them consider what might have been the lingering effects of West's departure from the script.

LOOKING TO THE FUTURE

Have students do some research into a possible career field that they're interested in, for example, sales, or teaching, or medicine. Ask them to find out the sorts of tasks or jobs that someone in such a career engages in over the course of a day: these might range from going on sales calls, to meeting with staff members, writing reports, answering email, etc. Once students have identified the tasks, ask them to write down the specific oral communication activities that will be engaged in while doing these jobs. For example, will this professional be speaking to groups? To a coworker? Phoning clients? Giving speeches? Addressing a courtroom or judge? Giving a sales pitch? Instructing a class? For each oral communication activity noted, ask students to consider the language style required for the task: What level of formality is needed for each? Finally, have students brainstorm ideas for how a person interested in entering such a career might go about strengthening his/her language skills.

Obviously an interview, either in person or via phone/email, with someone actually working in a particular career field would be helpful to your students as they research this assignment. They might also find these on-line sources beneficial as well:

About.com *Career Planning*: http://careerplanning.about.com/od/occupations/a/career_briefs.htm

About.com *Careers A to Z: Profiles, Quizzes and Personal*: http://careerplanning.about.com/od/careersatoz/Careers-A-To-Z-Profiles-Quizzes-Personal-Stories-And-Related-Occupations.htm

Career OneStop *Explore Careers*: http://careeronestop.org/ExploreCareers/ExploreCareers.aspx

SUGGESTED FURTHER READING

Language Processing

Aitchion, J. (2008). *The articulate mammal* (5th ed.). London: Routledge. The latest edition of an established bestseller, this text is an introduction to the discipline of psycholinguistics, covering topics which include language processing in the brain, language acquisition, and universal grammars.

Brownell, J. (2009). *Listening: Attitudes, principles, and skills* (4th ed.). Boston: Allyn and Bacon. This is the latest edition of Brownell's theories on listening, a process she suggests that involves six interrelated components. The book includes discussion and exercises on ways to improve one's listening processing.

Adapting Speech

Eckert, P. and Rickford, J. R. (2001). *Style and sociolinguistic variation.* Cambridge: Cambridge University Press. This collection of essays by leading scholars examines a range of approaches, including genre, social meaning, self-identification, and situational meaning, as well as studying stylistic variation in oral speech.

Knestrict, T. and Schoensteadt, L. (2005). Teaching social register and code switching in the classroom: Social skills instruction for children in poverty. *Journal of Children & Poverty 11*(2), 177–185. This article describes the curriculum of a middle school in Cincinnati, Ohio, that teaches children to decode and use a variety of American English registers, contextualizing this academic endeavor within current pedagogical and linguistic research.

Wolfram, W. and Schilling-Estes, N. (2006). Chapter 9: Dialects and style. *American English* (2nd ed.). Oxford: Blackwell. This text examines how variation in American English, across both time and geographical region, is intertwined with issues of identity, race, gender, power, privilege, and prestige. Chapter 9 focuses on style-shifting.

Chapter 4

Writing

College and Career Readiness
Anchor Standards for Writing

Text Types and Purposes

1. Write arguments to support claims in an analysis of substantive topics or texts, using valid reasoning and relevant and sufficient evidence.
2. Write informative/explanatory texts to examine and convey complex ideas and information clearly and accurately through the effective selection, organization, and analysis of content.
3. Write narratives to develop real or imagined experiences or events using effective technique, well-chosen details, and well-structured event sequences.

Production and Distribution of Writing

4. Produce clear and coherent writing in which the development, organization, and style are appropriate to task, purpose, and audience.
5. Develop and strengthen writing as needed by planning, revising, editing, rewriting, or trying a new approach.
6. Use technology, including the Internet, to produce and publish writing and to interact and collaborate with others.

Research to Build and Present Knowledge

7. Conduct short as well as more sustained research projects based on focused questions, demonstrating understanding of the subject under investigation.
8. Gather relevant information from multiple print and digital sources, assess the credibility and accuracy of each source, and integrate the information while avoiding plagiarism.
9. Draw evidence from literary or informational texts to support analysis, reflection, and research.

Range of Writing

10. Write routinely over extended time frames (time for research, reflection, and revision) and shorter time frames (a single sitting or a day or two) for a range of tasks, purposes, and audiences.

Teaching students to write effectively has long been one of the overarching goals of K-12 education and still is today, even though the tools and media used in writing are changing. Students know that they'll need good writing skills for academic success, but they may not know how important writing is to the business world. According to a survey commissioned by the College Board, "two-thirds of salaried workers in large U.S. companies have jobs that require writing" and the higher the position within a company, the more writing that individual will have to produce. One respondent reported, "Writing skills are fundamental in business. It's increasingly important to be able to convey content in a tight, logical, direct manner, particularly in a fast-paced technological environment" (National Commission on Writing, 2004, p. 3). So to enable students to meet the differing needs of both their academic and professional careers, the Anchor Standards for Writing identify three broad text types and/or purposes—argument, information/explanation, and narration—to help students learn to write *for a range of tasks, purposes, and audiences* (Standard #10).

TEXT TYPES AND PURPOSES

Some might question why the Anchor Standards identify only three specific purposes and/or text types for students to master when writing is recognized as a crucial skill in the modern Information Age. Don't students need to master a wide range of documents to become successful adults? In fact, the Anchor Standards enable teachers to keep their learning outcomes as relevant as possible for every student, regardless of their future education or career path. Rather than being forced to teach a "laundry list" of documents, genres, organizational structures, and so on, instruction can instead focus on language use itself through the study of rhetoric, that is, the study of how humans use language to accomplish specific purposes. In this way, rather than having their knowledge confined to limited, static forms, students will be able to analyze future rhetorical situations and, accordingly, make the most appropriate language choices in their writing.

For an example as to why the skill of rhetorical analysis plays such a crucial role in the writing process, think about how texting and tweeting are becoming central to communication in American business. Now just imagine the success of a new employee who texts a client the same way she texts her *bff* from high school! Our students must be prepared to fit each document they write to its specific context, enabling them to write effectively in their future academic and professional careers. As Anchor Standard #4 states, students must learn to make *the development, organization, and style . . . [of each document they produce] appropriate to task, purpose, and audience.*

But students find dealing with concrete textual features, like word choice or spelling, much easier to grasp than the intangible concepts underlying rhetorical analysis. To help students understand these concepts, Table 4.1 contrasts basic rhetorical aspects of the three text type categories to illustrate how the tangible and intangible aspects of language use function together. Organizational sections, for instance, are much more tangible than the underlying organizational principle, but without understanding the principle, a writer will not be able to effectively produce a new work. Table 4.1 also illustrates the flexibility of the Anchor Standards' text types and purposes. Each category of writing can stand on its own or be combined with the other(s) in a wide variety of ways to meet the needs of specific situations.

Table 4.1 Basic Rhetorical Aspects of the Writing Standards' Text Types

	Narration	Information	Argumentation
Example genres from academia and business	Historical account Biography/ Autobiography Prose fiction	Annual Report Medical research report Resumé	Business proposal Campaign ads Literary analysis
Organizing principle	Chronology	Exposition	Persuasion
Commonly used organizational sections	Setting Inciting moment Developing conflict Concluding moment	Introduction Thesis Evidential support Conclusion	Claim Reasons Objections & rebuttal Evidence Conclusion
Writer's purpose	Establishing a chronological perspective on subject	Teaching own expertise through text	Persuading reader to agree with a specific position
Reader's perspective	Sees time passing through writer's point of view	Learns from writer	Changes mind as a result of writer's work
Commonly used words and phrases	Words indicating time, time passing, or time that has passed	Words (not just adjectives) providing concrete details and how details link together	Words indicating how concepts connect to the writer's position, that is, pro or con

Standards

1. Write arguments to support claims in an analysis of substantive topics or texts, using valid reasoning and relevant and sufficient evidence.
2. Write informative/explanatory texts to examine and convey complex ideas and information clearly and accurately through the effective selection, organization, and analysis of content.
3. Write narratives to develop real or imagined experiences or events using effective technique, well-chosen details, and well-structured event sequences.
10. Write routinely over extended time frames (time for research, reflection, and revision) and shorter time frames (a single sitting or a day or two) for a range of tasks, purposes, and audiences.

EXERCISE 4.1

To help students analyze the connections between a text and its rhetorical context, ask them to apply the generalizations in Table 4.1 to their own specific reading and writing experiences. Begin by reviewing the table with them. Then give the students at least 5 minutes to read through it again on their own and think of specific examples for each of the three categories. For example, students might think of their own reading assignments, such as a short story or a textbook chapter, as well as their own writing assignments, like a historical analysis or a lab report, in addition to texts they've encountered outside of the classroom, for example a job ad or a magazine article. Then, as a class, work through the whole chart, tracing an example for each category through individual boxes to make sure the students understand how context and text are interconnected, regardless of the category.

Exercise Extension

Choose an example text for one of the Writing Standards' text type categories that your students have recently read. Then ask them how the context and text would have to change to ensure that the text belongs to a new category. For example, your students might have recently read *The Declaration of Independence*, an argumentative text. What would have to change to make this a narrative text? The audience? The organization? The language? What content would have to be added or removed? And so on. If time permits, you could even ask the students to draft a representative paragraph or two illustrating the new text type.

EXERCISE 4.2

The following scenarios ask students to make choices about text type based on specific rhetorical situations. Some situations may require a combination of these types. By focusing on the intended audience's needs/expectations in each situation, students should be able to determine the writer's role, purpose/text type(s), intended audience, general content. Depending on previous class assignments, you might even ask students to identify the appropriate formality level of the language. Table 4.2 provides a guide for your students to follow. Use the Guided Questions for Class Discussion below as a guide.

A. A student in a college psychology class is assigned to write an essay in which he reports to his classmates about recent research discoveries.
B. Following corporate policy, a salesclerk is asked to write the minutes from the monthly staff meeting at a specific store.
C. A candidate for president makes a campaign speech at a rally open to the general public.
D. A grandmother decides to write an autobiography for her grandchildren.
E. A teenager applies for her first job.
F. A new graduate applies to a bank for a business loan to open a new shoe store.

Table 4.2 Rubric for Exercise 4.2

	Writer's Role	Writer's Purpose	Intended Audience	General Content	Formality Level	Text Type
A. Student						
B. Salesclerk						
C. Candidate						
D. Grandmother						
E. Teenager						
F. Graduate						

Guided Questions for Class Discussion

1. Ask your students what role each writer plays in each scenario. What is motivating the writer?
2. Have students identify the intended audience for each scenario. What sort of language will the audience be expecting the writer to use? Informal? Formal? Why?
3. What would happen if a writer chose to use language that departed from the expectations of the audience? How would the audience react? Ask students to give some examples of inappropriate language for each scenario.

GENRE

Even though the Anchor Standards identify only three text types and/or purposes, asking students to memorize exact formats for writing in each category may limit the types of writing they produce, rather than allow them to use the categories as a foundation for all future writing assignments. To avoid limiting students in this way, instructors may want to guide students to a linguistic understanding of *genre*, which will help them comprehend how to make appropriate language choices for each document they write. Such a focus on *genre* may mean updating the term's definition for them.

In past decades, genre was considered a static classification system of written forms; students learned the forms and when to apply them, and then *poof*—good writers. Conceiving of genre exclusively as a form, however, handicaps writers rather than truly helping them use language effectively. Those who study and teach writing have realized that *genre* responds to recurring social, rhetorical contexts, and thus changes and adapts to meet each individual situation. As Amy Devitt (1993) explains, instead of focusing exclusively on the form of a text, the "effects," we should be looking to the "sources of those effects" (p. 573). Devitt and other researchers consider genre, then, to be "a rhetorical and essentially semiotic social construct" (p. 573). Every piece of writing exists within a larger, social exchange: for an example, go back to the instance of the young employee using the same language in her text messages at work as she uses in messages with her friends. If she thought about the rhetorical situation rather than just about the medium, she'd realize that more respectful, and more complete, language is needed for her workplace, for people who don't know her personally and who have the power to hire/fire her. Because she focused only on the form created by the medium, she erred grievously in her professional communication.

Interest in genre theory and the application of genre-based writing pedagogy began expanding in the 1980s. These approaches are generally considered more complete than earlier writing theories because they connect both text form and content with the rhetorical context addressed by a particular text. At least two different traditions developed almost simultaneously: the New Rhetoric, established by scholars in North America whose research primarily focused on university-level teaching in fields such as rhetoric and composition studies; and the Sydney School, developed by scholars in Australia who concerned themselves with primary and secondary school pedagogy.

Previously, writing pedagogy had tended to focus exclusively on the process of producing a text, with students drafting and revising, and teachers facilitating the process. But teachers and linguists working with Australian students learning English as a second language became concerned about the weaknesses they perceived in teaching process writing. Primary school students were writing primarily personal/ expressive narratives using their home language, leaving them unprepared for the more analytical and expository writing expected of them at the secondary level and beyond. And because the instructors' primary role in teaching process writing was as facilitators rather than as authoritative conveyors of knowledge about the formal textual elements, students who had not been exposed to standard or academic Englishes before entering school, like these Australian English language learners, were unable to learn the conventions of such important styles. In the words of J. R. Martin (2009):

> This limited experience of writing did very little to prepare students for learning across the curriculum in primary school, for writing in the specialized subject areas of secondary school, or for dealing with various community genres they might encounter as the most fluent English speaker of their family.
>
> (p. 11)

Because this exclusive focus on process writing was failing to provide students with all the language tools they needed to be successful, pedagogy based on genre theory began appearing in Australian classrooms.

After the initial success of applying genre theory in a limited number of class-rooms, educators in Australia expanded the practice, first in primary schools and then in secondary ones, as a way to provide inexperienced students a means of understanding and then writing successfully in new genres (Martin, 2009). The Australian success with genre theory models in school systems encouraged peda-gogical application of genre theory in the United States, as well as in other parts of the world.

Over time, with increasing research, the boundary lines between the different genre theory traditions have become blurred. In general, all approaches encourage teachers to first help their students analyze genre models, leading students to identify

Figure 4.1 Applying Genre Theory in the Classroom (Adapted from Martin (2009))

the recurrent features of the text (structure, format, lexicon, etc.), as well as recurrent features of the rhetorical situations (purpose, audience, exigency, etc.) in which this genre is appropriate. Next, the teacher and students work together to produce a sample text within the genre. Finally, each student works independently to produce his/her own, genre document. (See Figure 4.1.)

Throughout any genre study, teachers help students focus on the context that determines the text. For example, a writer might be familiar with the genre of business letters because of the frequent need for fairly brief communication between individuals/companies in the business world. But thinking of a business letter exclusively in terms of prescribed textual features prevents a writer from adapting those features to be appropriate to each unique rhetorical situation. Making a complaint, for instance, differs drastically from placing an order. The Anchor Standards for Writing encourage teachers to guide students in situating every writing task within its social, rhetorical context. Such an approach keeps writing authentic and helps students understand how genre conventions alter to meet the changes in specific situations.

Standards

4. Produce clear and coherent writing in which the development, organization, and style are appropriate to task, purpose, and audience.
10. Write routinely over extended time frames (time for research, reflection, and revision) and shorter time frames (a single sitting or a day or two) for a range of tasks, purposes, and audiences.

EXERCISE 4.3

This exercise models, in four steps, the process of genre analysis that students can apply to any rhetorical situation—academic, professional, personal—in which they might find themselves and so reinforces the concept that all textual choices are driven by the rhetorical situation. (Depending on the amount of experience your students have with textual analysis and/or on the amount of class time you have available, you could combine steps 1, 2, and 3 and so move more quickly through the analysis to the actual student writing.) The exercise asks you to choose a model genre for students to examine. Because this is an introduction to the genre-analysis process, choose a genre brief enough, such as want ads, personal advice columns, weather

Table 4.3 Rubric for Exercise 4.3

Genre Examples	Purpose	Intended Audience	Exigency	Structure	Tone	Format	Type of Vocabulary	Syntax
#1								
#2								
#3								
#4								
#5								
Shared features								

forecasts, letters to the editor, etc., that students can easily compare/contrast several examples of it at the same time. Table 4.3 provides a guide to help students with their analysis.

Step 1: Give students several examples of your chosen genre, for example a weather forecast from a newspaper, an on-line weather info site, a surfing site, etc., and ask them first to identify features of each example's rhetorical situation (purpose, intended audience, exigency, etc.) and then to identify those features shared in common. To help guide their analysis, possible questions include:

• Who is the intended audience for this document? How can you tell?
• Why was the document written? What's the purpose behind it?
• How does the rhetorical situation shape the writer's message?
• Why did the writer choose this particular medium (print or electronic) for this particular audience?

Step 2: Working with the same examples as in Step 1, ask students to identify the formal characteristics of each text (structure, format, lexicon, syntax, etc.) and then to identify those characteristics shared in common among all the texts. To help guide their analysis, possible questions include:

• What's the organization of the text? That is, how does it begin? What sort of information is in the middle? How does it end?
• What sort of tone does the text have? Personal? Formal? Detached? Involved?
• What is the text about? What sort of content does it have?
• How does the text appear on the page? What's the format? Does it have headings? A list? Paragraphs? Spacing? Etc.
• What sort of words does the text use? Formal? Easy? Jargon?
• What sorts of sentences are used? Are they long? Short? Is there a certain kind of punctuation used or one that is lacking?

Step 3: Ask students to analyze the relationship between the rhetorical situations that are shared in common and the formal characteristics of these texts that are shared in common. For example, why do weather reports always include future tense verbs? Why is the second person *you* appropriate for a complete stranger to use in a personal advice column? Why are word and sentence fragments appropriate in a want ad? And so on. Students need to understand how and why contexts shape texts so that they'll be able to adapt their own writing appropriately for future situations. To help guide their analysis, possible questions include:

- Why is this particular vocabulary appropriate for the intended audience?
- How does this format help the intended audience understand the content?
- How does beginning and ending in this way help the reader understand the purpose of the document?
- What seem to be the unique characteristics of this genre? How are they appropriate for the rhetorical situation?

Step 4: Give students a specific rhetorical situation appropriate for the genre that you've been using in the previous parts of this exercise, and ask them to write a text in response. For example, if you're working with weather forecasts, the rhetorical situation might be that a local TV station forecaster wants to warn viewers about a dangerous thunderstorm that's approaching. At this point, students should be able to identify the formal characteristics appropriate for a specific rhetorical situation and then incorporate them into an appropriate text. Remember that the point of genre theory is to focus on the social context rather than on rigid formulas. Effective writers adapt genre conventions to each unique situation rather than applying exactly the same precise formula over and over again.

Exercise Extension

Now choose a longer type of text that students can analyze on their own or within small groups: lab reports, sports articles, business letter complaints, etc. Be sure to give the students several written examples so that they can analyze the shared features of the rhetorical situation as well as the formal characteristics of the text. And you should know that most genre-theory pedagogy recommends working with students to fulfill a particular genre, such as a literary analysis or a position paper, before asking them to write in the genre on their own. Thus the students will have a model for the process that they can then apply on their own.

Guided Questions for Class Discussion

1. What contextual elements do these genre examples share? Audience? Topic? Purpose?
2. What textual characteristics does this context demand? Formal language? Jargon? Visual aids? Research data? And so on.
3. Does this genre fit within a single text category (narrative, informative, argumentative) or does it combine several together? Why or why not?

Standards

5. Develop and strengthen writing as needed by planning, revising, editing, rewriting, or trying a new approach.
10. Write routinely over extended time frames (time for research, reflection, and revision) and shorter time frames (a single sitting or a day or two) for a range of tasks, purposes, and audiences.

EXERCISE 4.4

For any writing assignment, students should always be able to explain their language choices in terms of the real-world rhetorical context they're addressing. This exercise asks students to analyze an existing document as well as their own revision of it. Ask students to convert a well-known piece of literature into another genre that they've already analyzed. For example, they could convert *The Declaration of Independence* into a want ad, *Hamlet* into a biography, *Letter from Birmingham Jail* into a personal advice column, and so on. Achieving success with this assignment means carefully analyzing both genres to understand the conventions of each. Students should include an analysis page that identifies important elements of the rhetorical situation of both documents and explains the reasoning behind their language choices in the final document itself. A sample analysis page appears in Figure 4.2.

Directions: Fill out the table below, identifying the language choices made to change a document from one genre to another. Then, below the chart, explain why you made these particular choices.

	Original Document	*New Document*
Purpose		
Intended audience		
Format		
Structure		
Vocabulary		
Tone		
Syntax		

Rationale for these changes:

Figure 4.2 Sample Cover Page for Exercise 4.4

As the previous discussion and series of exercises make clear, using genre theory in the classroom enables teachers to help students develop a linguistic knowledge of how effective language works. Such knowledge helps students because it makes learning goals concrete. Rather than saying things like "this is a good paragraph because it flows," a teacher can say "this is a good paragraph because it clearly explains the information a reader needs to know in x context." And it also creates assessment criteria, such as making choices about tone, syntax, and diction appropriate for the intended audience, that are portable from one writing assignment to another, lessening or even eliminating the perception that evaluating writing is totally subjective (Wyatt-Smith, 1997). When teachers introduce writing assignments by exploring the context, students will learn to expect assessments based on how well a final document fulfills the needs of that same context.

Genre and Rhetorical Moves

Using genre theory to examine the relationship between text and social context may also provide students a new and useful perspective through which to understand the concept of structure. Because they're working with intangible ideas, inexperienced students have a difficult time understanding the relationship between content and form, tending to use a mechanical structure for every piece of writing, whether that structure is appropriate or not. For example writing instructors commonly model the *5-paragraph theme* for their classes as a way to teach basic concepts of essay structure, intending students to build on that base as their writing skills expand. (See Figure 4.3.) But some students are unable to leave that tangible model. They find the task of writing a required paper longer than the *5-paragraph theme* impossible to do because they truly don't understand that content and form work together. Instead these students try to impose the same 5-paragraph form on every document (Wesley, 2000). Genre theory asks that writers think about each element of their developing text in terms of the rhetorical situation. So rather than focusing on vague units, like the introduction or the body, which doesn't provide assistance for inexperienced students, writers instead think about *rhetorical moves*, specific cognitive structures that are used across a genre to organize information and help fulfill the overall purpose of the text.

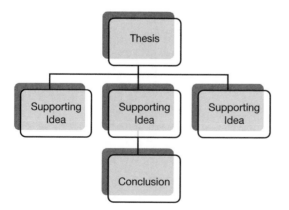

Figure 4.3 Structure of the Traditional 5-paragraph Theme

John Swales (1981) illustrated the usefulness of this type of analysis in his study of the scientific research article genre, which quantitatively identified the three rhetorical moves of the genre's introduction, as well as the possible steps for fulfilling each move. (See Figure 4.4.) As professional academics know, and as students do not know, getting a research article published is highly competitive. Before considering any article, an editor will want to know how it fits into current published research as well as what new information it presents. Swales' three moves clearly address that context.

Move 1: Identifies Field by indicating importance of field and/or making topic generalizations about field and/or reviewing previous research in field

Move 2: Identifies Individual Position within Field by making a specific claim or raising a question or continuing a tradition

Move 3: Explains Plan to Fulfill Individual Position by outlining purposes or announcing present research or indicating following article's structure

---

Figure 4.4 The CARS (Create a Research Space) Model for Writing Academic Introductions (Adapted from Swales (1981))

As you can see, a student and/or researcher who's never written in this genre before has a clear outline of the three different "moves" present in a research article introduction, as well as some suggestions for how to fulfill each move. If writers understand these moves, they will be less likely to make the common student mistake of simply summarizing what has already been written on the topic, and will focus instead on describing their addition to the existing knowledge. Following Swales' example model, numerous studies have been published examining the rhetorical moves of a wide variety of genres in professional writing, including business reports, medical narratives, and academic writing.

EXERCISE 4.5

Asking students to identify moves can be extremely challenging because they must focus on the movement of ideas within paragraphs, not just on the paragraphs themselves. So to help students understand the concept of rhetorical moves, for this exercise students will analyze two different introductions to research articles to understand how Swales' CARS model provides a helpful guide.

First explain the CARS model to your students, being sure that they understand the rhetorical context and how the moves described fulfill that context. Then give each student the two article introductions below and ask them to determine if Swales' model fits each individual introduction. They'll need to identify the sentence(s) that satisfy each move and be able to explain why.

Example 1:

In the United States, asthma is the leading cause of morbidity in children and is presently the most commonly reported cause of school absenteeism, accounting for one-third of all days missed of instruction (Boice, 1998). Educators have recognized that students with serious health needs are at risk for academic failure. School health services personnel play a supportive role for students with asthma through the promotion of wellness, while aiding in achieving adequate asthma control through self-management skills. For students with asthma, the time spent in the health office attending to medical needs is often at the expense of classroom instruction, participation in physical education classes, or engagement in social activities. Much of the health care process may depend on the student's attitude toward absenteeism and his or her perception of the school health personnel as agents of change. The underlying assumption is that school nurses serve as a resource for stress reduction and social support, advocate for a trigger-free environment, and are a reliable resource for medical care.

The purpose of this study was to compare the relationship between students with asthma to students without asthma regarding attitudes toward school health services, absenteeism, school nurse support for participation in extracurricular activities, student academic achievement in mathematics and English, and days absent.

(Krenitsky-Korn, 2011, p. 61)

Example 2:

High school students, and particularly girls, are not very active (Centers for Disease Control and Prevention, 2006). To help girls develop the abilities to enjoy lifetime, healthy physical activity, physical educators need to provide curricula that will achieve this goal. In the process, they need to make sure they are aligned with the current trends and interests of their students. Fitness activities such as Pilates, kickboxing, and core training have become popular at fitness centers and some physical educators are incorporating them into their curricula. There is a lack of research examining students' views of these activities. This study examined 83 high school girls' perceptions of selected fitness activities, after participating in several fitness units. From the students' comments, 74% of the girls preferred fitness units to sports units. Eight themes were identified from student comments showing that students found the fitness activities to be: health-promoting, fun and varied, more physically active, easier skills than sports, good lifetime activities, easy to schedule outside of school, a help in increasing other abilities, and not competitive. The findings reinforce the need for high school physical educators to include such activities as options in their high school curricula to motivate girls to be more active.

(Wilkinson and Bretzing, 2011, p. 58)

Guided Questions for Class Discussion

1. Compare/contrast the rhetorical moves of these two introductions by exploring how each author makes his/her niche possess value. What's unique about it, and why would anyone care?

2. Compare/contrast the intended audience of each introduction. Who are these readers, and how is the language/content used appropriate for each audience?
3. Academic publications are extremely competitive, so authors have to identify how their work is more significant than or superior to others' research. How does the language/content of these introductions address that purpose?
4. What expectation does each introduction set for the rest of the article? What will readers expect to find?
5. What sort of changes would make these introductions more appropriate for a newspaper article intended for the general public?

Although giving students a template, such as the CARS model, to follow when first teaching a genre can be quite useful because of all the information a template can quickly convey, teachers need to be aware of a potential problem. Focusing exclusively on the text being produced, such as a template does, may actually handicap students in the future. To keep their writing effective, students need to understand how each text always fulfills a particular rhetorical situation, so any use of templates always needs to be tied to an individual context. The following exercise expands the students' analysis of introductions from the previous exercise by asking them to consider genres other than scientific research articles.

EXERCISE 4.6

Give students the introductions to documents belonging to two other genres than the scientific research article with which they are now familiar, such as a film review, an editorial, driving directions, etc. Then ask them to complete the following steps, either through a class discussion or through a written assignment.

1. Ask students to compare/contrast the rhetorical situations with that of Swales' CARS model. How are the audiences, audience expectations, and writers' purposes similar, and how are they different?
2. Ask students to determine if the CARS model describes these non-academic introductions too. How are they similar, and how are they different?
3. Ask students how each introduction is appropriate for its own rhetorical context.

Guided Questions for Class Discussion

1. Ask students to compare/contrast specific elements of each genre. For example, how is the word choice in one document different from the other? Sentence length? Types of sentences? And so on. Students should be able to discuss how each of these elements is appropriate for the intended audience.
2. Based on the introduction, what do students expect from the rest of the document?

3. Ask students to identify ways to revise one introduction to make it appropriate for the rhetorical context of the other document. If you have time, you might even ask the students to complete this as a writing assignment.

Genre and Medium

Because writers today have access to a much wider array of media than in previous periods, students need to think about choosing the appropriate medium when considering their genre options to ensure that they're making the most effective choices possible. And they need to be aware that the medium is not the same thing as the genre, an error that inexperienced writers frequently make. One can send a formal email, for example, or an informal letter. Each medium contains a wide variety of genres. And complicating this issue is the rapid development of new media in our digital age and the changing cultural attitudes as each one becomes widely available. Students need to think rhetorically about media choices so that they'll be prepared to work appropriately in whatever new media become available in the future.

Standards

6. Use technology, including the Internet, to produce and publish writing and to interact and collaborate with others.
10. Write routinely over extended time frames (time for research, reflection, and revision) and shorter time frames (a single sitting or a day or two) for a range of tasks, purposes, and audiences.

EXERCISE 4.7

The following rhetorical situations illustrate inappropriate choices of writing mediums for each rhetorical situation. Ask students to explain why these media choices are inappropriate and suggest a more appropriate choice. Once they've worked through these examples, ask them to draw generalizations about each medium that could guide other writers. When is an email appropriate, for example, versus a paper document versus a text message?

1. A husband of 6 years announces on Twitter that he wants a divorce from his wife.
2. A new employee emails her boss to ask where the employee restrooms are.
3. A man invites his neighbors to come over after dinner to watch football by sending a letter through the mail.
4. A clothing store announces its changing hourly specials through postcards.
5. A recent graduate sends a text message to a CEO asking for a job.

Guided Questions for Class Discussion

1. What audience would be appropriate for each of these media? (A close friend or partner, a single individual, a small group, a large group, an unknown reader, etc.)
2. How would a reader use each of these media forms? (Save for future reference, read once and destroy, pass on information to other readers, etc.)
3. What sort of content would be easy to understand in each medium? (Many specific details, numbers and data, brief overview, command to do something, announcement, etc.)
4. What would be the response of someone who actually received one of the messages as described above?

EXERCISE 4.8

This exercise asks students to think about revising a document from one medium/ genre to another, forcing them to literally "re-see" their own writing. After students have written an essay assignment of any kind for your class, or perhaps for a class in another discipline, ask them to reflect on how they would change it to make it appropriate for a web page.

1. Begin with a discussion of conventions: What's the matter with just posting the essay as they've already written it on-line? How would readers respond?
2. Ask students to identify the conventions of web pages that aren't present in their own academic essays. Why do those conventions exist? What's different about the audience and purpose of web pages from those of academic essays?
3. Ask students to write a plan for revising their essay for a web page, detailing the changes they would make. For example, if they'd add headings, what headings would they add? Where would the headings go? What sort of illustrations? Where would they go? How would sentences and paragraphs change? And so on.

Exercise Extension

If you have time, have the students actually write the revision, producing the pages of their web site. This could be done on paper if you don't have easy access or technical support for the students to create actual web pages.

Genre and Sources

Using a genre-based approach provides students with a new perspective on learning about integrating source material into their own writing as well as documenting it. Secondary schools focus primarily on teaching academic writing styles because that's what students need for immediate success at the high school level. And of course students need the knowledge and skills of academic writing styles to be successful in college. But documentation styles in academia have so many details that students have a difficult time perceiving that the intricacies fulfill the needs of a rhetorical context. In fact, they frequently don't even understand that a rhetorical context exists. So addressing documentation in terms of genre allows attention to detail but maintains the overall focus on the document's purpose and intended audience. After all, choices about documentation style are tied to specific genres. Social science research articles use a documentation style (APA) that fulfills the needs of their specific audience, while literary criticism uses a different style (MLA) tied to its audience's needs. Understanding the motivation underlying the details will help students recognize the choices that need to be made.

In addition, many times high school students will disregard direction and teaching about sources and documentation because they perceive this knowledge to be of no consequence in "the real world"; they don't think they'll ever use this knowledge/skill set once they leave school. The following exercise asking students to identify source use in non-academic genres directly attacks the idea that sources and documentation exist only in the academic world. And, of course, the rhetorical moves shaping the different genres vary in order to be appropriate for the intended audience and purpose of each document.

Standards

7. Conduct short as well as more sustained research projects based on focused questions, demonstrating understanding of the subject under investigation.
8. Gather relevant information from multiple print and digital sources, assess the credibility and accuracy of each source, and integrate the information while avoiding plagiarism.
9. Draw evidence from literary or informational texts to support analysis, reflection, and research.
10. Write routinely over extended time frames (time for research, reflection, and revision) and shorter time frames (a single sitting or a day or two) for a range of tasks, purposes, and audiences.

EXERCISE 4.9

Students frequently think that using sources is something that occurs only in academic writing. But a source is anything that provides information, whether an academic report on an experiment or an interview in a newspaper article. So asking students to identify the use of sources in the writing of everyday life can be a real eye-opener for them. This experience can help them to think about how and why writers use sources rather than to obsess over how many sources a particular assignment requires. Indicating how important the skill of incorporating source material is for students, 3 of the 10 Anchor Standards for Writing describe the relationship between writing and research.

To get students started, give them several different types of popular written genres that contain references. For example, you can easily find a newspaper article, a movie or music review, a sports article, etc.—even a teen magazine article uses sources. These genres are usually short enough that they could be read and analyzed in class, or they could be assigned as homework reading. Then, using the following guided questions, lead the students to consider how each genre uses source material. Table 4.4 provides a guide to help students with their analysis. You'll notice that the question at the end of the list asks students to compare/contrast academic genres with nonacademic genres. If students understand why they have to include particular details in their writing, they're much more likely to do so effectively.

Table 4.4 Rubric for Exercise 4.9

Genre Examples:	#1	#2	#3	#4
Intended audience				
Purpose				
Introduction of source				
Direct quote, summary, or paraphrase				
Type of source material				
Intended effect on reader				

Guided Questions for Class Discussion

1. What's the rhetorical context for each of these documents? Who's the intended reader, and what's the purpose of the writer?
2. How does each document introduce the source material? Does it indicate the writer, the speaker, the article title, or something else? Is there an explanation of who or what the source is? Is this appropriate for the rhetorical context?
3. Are quotation marks used to indicate direct quotes? Or is the information summarized or paraphrased? How does the style chosen fit the needs of the intended audience?
4. What type of source material is used? Is it an interview, an article, a book, a political document, etc.? Is this what a reader would expect to see in the particular genre? Would a reader expect to see any other types of sources that don't appear in this particular document?
5. Why is source material used? What's the effect on the reader? Why doesn't the author just rely exclusively on his/her own opinion and/or experiences?
6. Compare/contrast the use of sources in these nonacademic documents with academic writing. Why does nonacademic writing usually include only the source's name and the context of the information used (such as an interview or an article), while academic writing includes things like the page number, the publisher, etc.? How do the intended audiences differ? How will the intended audiences use the information the writer provides?

Exercise Extension

Give students another nonacademic scenario in which to consider the use of source material, but this time, place them in the position of the intended audience of a business document. For example, ask students to imagine that they work in a bank approving loans to help new businesses get started. What sort of information (product prices, wages, suppliers, profit margins, etc.) would they need to see in a business proposal/loan application to decide whether or not to loan the money? Where would the prospective business owner get this information from? How would the bank know that the information in the proposal/application is reliable? Other possible scenarios for this assignment include working in a Human Resources department screening applications, or a college admissions office making decisions about college applications. Students should see that both source material and documentation are essential elements in nonacademic, as well as academic, writing. The differences lie in the rhetorical moves shaping each genre.

MEETING STUDENTS WHERE THEY ARE

One genre that your students probably know extremely well, maybe even better than you do, is text messages. Because they've probably only sent and received text messages with friends, however, they may never have thought about the ways in which this genre adapts to fit different rhetorical situations. So the following exercise encourages them to understand that every document, no matter how short or informal it is, must meet the needs of a specific rhetorical context in order to be effective.

Begin by dividing students into small groups and asking them to write a list of the expectations, "the rules," they have for text messages, as well as the requirements imposed by the medium itself. For example, punctuation in a text message tends to be very different from that in SAE. Then bring the students back together and ask the whole class to define the rhetorical situation for their use of text messages: Who's the intended audience? What's the purpose? Do the rules they've identified meet the needs of the rhetorical context?

Next, return the class to their small groups and give them the following list of different scenarios in which a text message might be used. Then ask them how the language used in the text message might vary from one context to the next in order to be appropriate:

1. Telling a relative about an upcoming visit
2. Telling a boss you'll be late because of a car problem
3. Asking a fellow student you barely know for help with a homework assignment
4. Telling a regular customer that the store where you work is having a sale
5. Telling your best friend that you got an A on an exam

Finally, bring the class back together for a discussion of their analysis.

Guided Questions for Class Discussion

1. Ask students if they would use the same acronyms and abbreviations in each of these scenarios. Why or why not?
2. Would they use the same spelling and abbreviations in each of these scenarios? Why or why not?
3. How can they tell what language to use in each scenario? Is it the audience that determines language choices? The purpose? The message?
4. The whole reason for text-messaging is to be quick. Is there ever a time when a writer would use formal syntax, spelling, and punctuation in a text message?

Exercise Extension

Interview a teacher, a superior at work, or a parent about how text messaging is used in their profession/work world. What sorts of abbreviations and acronyms are used? What content is appropriate? How formal is tone? And so on. Students should learn the intended audience and the purpose for such texts as well as details about what language is used.

LOOKING TO THE FUTURE

To truly use language effectively in every situation, writers should always remember that it changes: tone, format, style, word choice, even spelling and punctuation change from one context to another. Students are already familiar with more recent punctuation conventions commonly used when texting a friend, but they may not have realized that even formal punctuation changes over time. Punctuation was first used in classical Greek times to indicate oral delivery of a passage—a long pause, a short pause, and so on. Then, during the 18th century, writers began using punctuation to indicate the syntactical relationships in a sentence. So rather than thinking about how a reader might recite a passage aloud, writers concerned themselves with helping readers read a passage to themselves by marking syntactical structures, such as appositives and coordinate clauses. For example, periods first appeared in manuscripts after each individual word to indicate the word's ending rather than after a full sentence; simply using a blank space to mark divisions between words came later.

Today many scholars have pointed out that modern writers use fewer marks of punctuation and simpler sentences than did writers of earlier periods. Just compare the following sentences to see how trends in punctuation are changing:

1. There are days which occur in this climate, at almost any season of the year, wherein the world reaches its perfection, when the air, the heavenly bodies, and the earth, make a harmony, as if nature would indulge her offspring; when, in these bleak upper sides of the planet, nothing is to desire that we have heard of the happiest latitudes, and we bask in the shining hours of Florida and Cuba; when everything that has life gives sign of satisfaction, and the cattle that lie on the ground seem to have great and tranquil thoughts.

(Emerson, "Essay VI," *Nature*, 1844, para. 1)

2. My bandanna is rolled on the diagonal and retains water fairly well. I keep it knotted around my head, and now and again dip it into the river. The water is forty-six degrees. Against the temples, it is refrigerant and relieving. This has done away with the headaches that the sun caused in days before. The Arctic sun—penetrating, intense—seems not so much to shine as to strike. Even the trickles of water that run down my T-shirt feel good. Meanwhile, the river— the clearest, purest water I have ever seen flowing over rocks—breaks the light into flashes and sends them upward into the eyes.

(McPhee, *Coming into the Country*, 1991, p. 5)

Scholars also speculate that the apostrophe will disappear from use in another century or so because it doesn't provide essential meaning to a sentence. And of course the new electronic medium of writing has introduced new marks of punctuation in emoticons. Every aspect of writing fulfills the needs of a specific rhetorical context.

Ask students to write about the role of emoticons in 100 years. Right now, they're only used in informal documents, and usually only between people who know each other. Will they be more widely accepted in 100 years and so used in formal writing too? All of them or just a few of them? Students should support their opinion with an analysis of the relationship between punctuation and reader expectations. Will emoticons provide essential information to readers in the future? Why aren't they widely used today and so accepted in formal writing?

SUGGESTED FURTHER READING

Text Types and Purposes

Hillocks, G. J. (2011). *Teaching argument writing, grades 6–12: Supporting claims with relevant evidence and clear reasoning*. Portsmouth, NH: Heinemann. Hillocks explores what argumentative writing is, as well as how to teach it effectively through real-life examples, suggested exercise ideas, and handouts. The discussion grows progressively more difficult, beginning with "arguments of facts" and ending with "arguments of judgments," but always stays focused on the intended audience of grades 6–12.

Genre

Dean, D. (2008). *Genre theory: Teaching, writing, and being*. Urbana, IL: NCTE. Dean explores the value of contemporary genre theory through application in the 9–12 grade classroom. In addition to suggesting student activities, Dean also discusses pedagogical practices and assessment.

Freedman, A. and Medway, P. (Eds.) (1994). *Learning and teaching genre*. Portsmouth, NH: Boynton/Cook. This collection of essays focuses on academic writing, at the high school and college levels, through the lens of genre theory. It explores how students learn genres and how teachers teach them, including discussions of subversion and resistance. The text also includes numerous examples of successful classroom practices.

Johns, A. M. (Ed.) (2001). *Genre in the classroom: Multiple perspectives*. Mahwah, NJ: Lawrence Erlbaum Associates. This collection of essays represents the varied theoretical perspectives on genre, describing through specific examples how those theories have shaped classroom practices. Its international scope provides authentic and diverse examples of the essential interconnections between theory and pedagogy.

Kress, G. (1999). Genre and the changing contexts for English language arts. *Language Arts* 76, 461–469. In this essay, Kress provides a brief overview of the debates between the various genre theory perspectives, as well as an overview of the theory itself. She argues that a social understanding of genre is necessary in reconfiguring the language arts so that they maintain their relevance.

Chapter 5

Reading

Being literate is universally acknowledged as perhaps the most essential skill a person can possess. Literacy not only empowers individuals by allowing them to be able to make decisions and control their own lives, but it also strengthens nations by helping to reduce poverty and inequality through education. In our current global, knowledge-based economy, being literate is no longer a choice but an imperative. In the last few decades, the definition of literacy has had to broaden to meet the needs of our changing world: while, in the past, literacy was defined as the ability to read and write a simple sentence, today its definition has expanded to include the capacity to understand, analyze, and use language adequately in diverse media for an array of communication purposes.

Responding to this broader definition of literacy, most language arts curricula today are designed to introduce students to a variety of informational and literary texts. While the broad exposure promotes higher levels of literacy, at the same time, students are often challenged by content and language that is unfamiliar to them. The authors of the Anchor Standards allude to these reading challenges when they note that to "become college and career ready, students must grapple with works of exceptional craft and thought whose range extends across genres, cultures, and centuries" (Note, College and Career Readiness Standards for Reading, p. 35). The authors' use of the word *grapple*, meaning "to come to grips" or "to wrestle," reflects their awareness of the challenges facing students who are assigned works written in diverse settings, locations, times, or even unfamiliar Englishes. At the same time, however, they recognize the importance of students becoming adept in a variety of reading situations. From having a firm grasp of the concepts in our country's founding documents, to knowing the ancient literatures that have shaped and expressed the human condition, to reading a set of instructions on a college or job application, today's students must be able to read and comprehend a wide range of texts. The following discussion will explore ways in which teachers can help students achieve this goal.

Researchers in reading and literacy have long argued that, for students to comprehend texts, they must have knowledge of the reading process and access to strategies for achieving greater reading comprehension. Although theories about how we construct meaning when we read vary in their specifics, most scholars today accept a general view of the reading process as an interaction between reader and text, in which readers are not merely receivers of textual meaning but creators of it (Goodman, 1996; Rosenblatt, 2005; Appleman, 2009). Readers apparently use prior knowledge, such as personal experience and cultural information, to derive meaning from what they read.

Research has shown the impact of personal experience and knowledge on reading comprehension: in well-known studies conducted in the 1970s, researchers gave purposely ambiguous reading passages to sets of readers who shared the same interests, hobbies, life experiences, and so on (Anderson, Reynolds, Schallert, and Goetz, 1977; Steffensen, Joag-Dev, and Anderson, 1979). Results of the studies showed that the readers' background experiences, or prior knowledge, heavily influenced their comprehension of a passage. Later research has added to these findings by broadening the definition of "prior knowledge" to include the understanding and usage of certain language patterns and modes of discourse. As Early and Ericson (1993) found, "Good readers anticipate words and phrases because they are familiar with how . . . language works, as well as with many of the ideas conveyed in that language" (p. 315). The research suggests then that a person's prior experience, including his/her linguistic knowledge, strongly affects reading comprehension. The implications of this research are significant when we consider the breadth and variety of texts students will encounter in their studies and beyond. Helping them to develop meta-cognitive awareness of their role in the reading process now will aid them in achieving greater reading comprehension in the texts they will encounter in the future. The following exercise demonstrates the critical role of the reader in creating meaning.

Standard

1. Read closely to determine what the text says explicitly and to make logical inferences from it; cite specific textual evidence when writing or speaking to support conclusions drawn from the text.

EXERCISE 5.1

Ask students to get into small groups and discuss the meanings of the headlines below, taken from actual news stories. As they work, ask them also to consider how they arrived at the meanings their group has decided on: How did they know what these headlines were referring to? Once the groups have had time to discuss the headlines, bring them together as a class and discuss their reading processes, using the guided discussion questions below.

Newspaper headlines:

1. RED TAPE HOLDS UP NEW BRIDGE
2. ARSON SUSPECT IS HELD IN MASSACHUSETTS FIRE
3. MAN JUMPS OFF BRIDGE; NEITHER JUMPER NOR BODY FOUND
4. SOMETHING WENT WRONG IN JET CRASH, EXPERT SAYS
5. HUNTER THROWS BUCK INTO POT FOR CHARITY

Guided Questions for Class Discussion

1. Ask your students to explain why ambiguity occurs in each of these headlines.
2. Are students able to rearrange the syntax (word order) in some of the headlines to make the intended meaning clearer?
3. Ask students to consider the cultural knowledge needed in order to correctly understand some of the headlines. For example, some of the words and phrases have more than one meaning or varied connotations.
4. What do your students think the news article accompanying each headline will be about?

The student groups examining the headlines in Exercise 5.1 probably arrived at very similar meanings, despite the headlines' ambiguities. You might point out to the class that they were able to come up with similar answers not just because they understood the words they were reading—after all, many of them were ambiguous—but also because they drew on their cultural and linguistic knowledge in order to create meaning. So, for instance, to understand headline #1, students had to be familiar with the English language idiom *red tape* in order to make sense of it. Headlines #2 and #5 also require linguistic knowledge: the words *held* and *buck* are homonyms, that is, that they contain two or more unrelated meanings, and therefore students had to make an appropriate choice of meaning while reading. Number 5 requires the reader to have cultural knowledge of, or experience with, ways in which contributions are solicited, in this case perhaps by putting money in when something is passed around, or maybe buying a chance to win a drawing. The exercise demonstrates that students use much more than vocabulary recognition to understand texts: like all readers, they rely on linguistic and cultural knowledge for comprehension. This knowledge enables readers not only to create meaning but also to anticipate what is to come, another essential step in the reading process. Students were probably very capable of predicting the content of the news stories following the headlines in the exercise above.

MAKING PERSONAL CONNECTIONS TO TEXTS

Another way to get students to actively engage in meta-cognition about the reading process is suggested by educator Deborah Appleman (2009), who proposes that they consider reading as an interaction between themselves and the text. Using concepts first articulated in reader-response literary theory, she talks about the "transaction," or interaction, that takes place between reader and text, which helps readers to create individual responses to a work. Figure 5.1, based on Appleman's model, illustrates the interaction occurring during the reading process. Having students consult this figure as they encounter unfamiliar texts may be helpful in getting them to think about their role in the reading process.

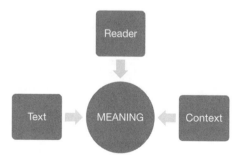

Figure 5.1 Interactions between Reader and Text Create Individual Responses (Adapted from Appleman (2009))

Standards

2. Determine central ideas or themes of a text and analyze their development; summarize the key supporting details and ideas.
3. Analyze how and why individuals, events, and ideas develop and interact over the course of a text.

EXERCISE 5.2

Step 1: Hand out a copy of Figure 5.1, or draw it on the board and review with students their roles as readers. Next, give students an unfamiliar work, such as a poem or short, short story, which they can read in a few minutes of class time and ask them to read through it silently. The example used here is Shelley's "Ozymandias" (found at http://www.potw.org/archive/potw46.html) but any short text of your choice will work.

Step 2: After they've read the text, ask students to jot down personal characteristics of theirs that they feel might be relevant to their reading of the text. For the example here, students might think about monuments they have seen or perhaps their awareness of the breakdown through time of structures supposedly meant to "last forever." Their examples might range from seeing crumbling WWI memorials in their hometown, to experiencing the shuttering of a family company, neighborhood store, or other favorite hangout. They might also consider great leaders, or other people they know of, who have "fallen" from a place of importance, either because of the passage of time, because of scandal, or for some other reason. Next, ask students to write down the textual properties that shape their understanding. These might be aspects such as vocabulary, punctuation, speaker, tone, etc. They should consider only those elements that affect their reading. In "Ozymandias," for instance, they might note unfamiliar words, such as *trunkless*, *visage*, and *boundless*. Or they might comment on the difficulty of finding the beginning and end of sentences, and thus whole thoughts, in the work.

Step 3: Ask students to write in their own words two or three ideas that they feel the poem expresses. What ideas is the speaker in the poem trying to convey? Once students have completed the written portion of the exercise, have them share their ideas about the poem's themes with the rest of the class. If you find that students' answers vary quite a bit, suggest to the class that this variation may be due to their personal connections to the poem and demonstrate this by asking them to share some of the ideas they jotted down regarding their personal connections to the text. The variety of connections should show how individual responses by readers help shape meanings in texts.

Step 4: As a last part of this exercise, ask students to think meta-cognitively. How might Figure 5.1 be useful in the future when they engage an unfamiliar text?

Guided Questions for Class Discussion

1. Ask your students if it was difficult for them to relate something from their personal experiences to the poem after having only read it by themselves and not discussed it as a class.
2. What particular words or phrases in the poem helped your students to think about personal experiences that may be relevant to the work?
3. Ask students what they did when they encountered an unfamiliar word. Did not knowing its meaning affect the way they understood the poem? Why or why not?
4. Discuss with your students times when they may have felt let down or betrayed by those whom they have admired or honored. Examples might include MLB all-time homerun record holder Barry Bonds, for instance, who since achieving his record has been linked to steroid use. Or perhaps your students have been dismayed by actions of politicians or other elected officials, whose reputations have been tainted, or who may have even been driven from office, by charges of malfeasance, corruption, infidelity, and so on. Can they relate their feelings about these "falls from power" to the situation described in "Ozymandias"? Ask them to discuss what similarities might exist between the fallen leader in this older poem and the dishonored persons in these more contemporary situations.

Students can refer to Figure 5.1 above when reading any kind of text, including those that are informational. In the exercise below, use the sample informational text, or one of your own choosing, to convey to your students how personal experience, combined with the text, constructs meaning.

EXERCISE 5.3

Following the format in Exercise 5.2 above, ask students to read the following passage and then note down any personal characteristics or experiences of theirs that they feel are relevant to the text. Next, they should list any textual properties that shape their understanding. Finally, they should write down two or three major concepts that the passage seems to express. As a last step, ask students to share their ideas with the rest of the class, and, if you desire, have them discuss the value of using Figure 5.1 in their reading process. Guided questions for discussion are below to aid you in your discussion.

From *Freakonomics*:

The Internet has proven particularly fruitful for situations in which a face-to-face encounter with an expert might actually exacerbate the problem of asymmetrical information—situations in which an expert uses his informational advantage to make us feel stupid or rushed or cheap or ignoble. Consider a scenario in which your loved one has just died and now the funeral director (who knows that you know next to nothing about his business and are under emotional duress to boot) steers you to the $8,000 mahogany casket. Or consider the automobile *dealership: a salesman does his best to obscure the car's base price under a mountain of add-ons and incentives. Later, however, in the cool-headed calm of your home, you can use the Internet to find out exactly how much the dealer paid for that car. Or you might just log on to TributeDirect.com and buy that mahogany casket yourself for only $3,595, delivered overnight. Unless you decide to spend $2,300 for "The Last Hole" (a casket with golf scenes) or "Memories of the Hunt" (featuring big-racked bucks and other prey) or one of the much cheaper models that the funeral director somehow failed even to mention.*

(Levitt and Dubner, 2009, p. 65)

Guided Questions for Class Discussion

1. Ask students if they have ever experienced the situation described above by Levitt and Dubner in which an expert made them feel dumb, hurried, cheap, etc. When did this occur and what kind of transaction was taking place? Why was this situation an example of "asymmetrical information"?
2. Why did Levitt and Dubner choose to use the examples of the funeral director and the car salesman to make their points? If students have never personally experienced such situations, could they still relate to these scenarios? Why or why not?
3. Ask students to consider how the Internet changes a situation of asymmetrical information.
4. Why might Levitt and Dubner have chosen to include the last two sentences in their paragraph? What do students think they add to the points they are trying to make?
5. Can students identify the main ideas in this paragraph and explain how they know this? What sort of knowledge are they bringing to the text, as readers, to determine this?

Exercise Extension

Find another type of informational text, different from that used in the exercise above. For instance, you could choose an advertisement, a bumper sticker, a campaign poster, or other text. Ask students to "read" the text at home, consciously thinking about their roles in the reading process. What personal experience, cultural knowledge, and linguistic information do they bring to their reading? Have students write a 2-paragraph response to the text: one paragraph that describes the main ideas they think the text is trying to convey, and another paragraph that describes their reading process.

MAKING MEANING FROM LANGUAGE

Asking students to find personal connections to texts is a worthwhile pedagogical tool . . . except when it doesn't work. Many of us have probably experienced the case when students fail to relate a text to their own lives and thus resist any discussion of it in class, leaving the teacher to provide explication. Texts that present this kind of situation are often those in which language usage is strange, arcane, and/or unfamiliar. Such usages are very common and appear, for example, in the plays of

Shakespeare or other works that use archaic Englishes, in informational works such as academic or technical articles that employ jargon-heavy discourse, and in literary works such as poems and novels that often contain lyrical language, diverse dialects, or literary tropes. The Anchor Standards for Reading recognize that adult readers today encounter a wide and diverse range of language usage in formats such as these, and thus they require that high school students be able to *interpret words and phrases as they are used in a text, including determining technical, connotative, and figurative meanings* . . . (Standard #4). While the benchmark is high—comprehension in all reading situations—students can achieve this goal if they are offered a variety of reading genres that employ a range of language usages. In the following discussion, we examine various usages and explore ways to help students become better readers by encouraging their meta-cognitive awareness of how language carries meaning.

When we teach new texts, we encourage students to create the frameworks for, or to contextualize, the speaker/narrator and his/her milieu. So, for example, instructors may discuss with their classes the 14th-century Italian ruling family structures that drive the action in Shakespeare's *Romeo and Juliet*, or the racial politics and prejudices of the mid-20th century that underlie Walter Dean Myers' *The Greatest, Muhammad Ali*. Instructor demonstration in class of researching and providing background information on a text provides students with an important tool that they can use later on when reading new texts on their own.

In addition to situating the period and setting, students should also be encouraged to contextualize the *language* of the text. Like the contextualization of time and place, the framing of textual *discourse* leads to greater student reading comprehension.

Contextualizing Discourse

The notion of "contextualizing discourse" originally derives from linguistic studies of oral and written communication in which the term "discourse" was used to describe any set of connected utterances or sentences, such as conversations, scripts, speeches, novels, and so on. Some of the research done by scholars in the field of discourse studies (Weatherall, Taylor, and Yates, 2001; Renkema, 2004) has shown that our spoken and written language tends to be highly ambiguous. Due to this ambiguity, both listeners and readers must continually make inferences about what they are hearing or reading in order to arrive at meaning. In other words, they must continually contextualize the language situation. Take for example a speech situation in which someone is told by a friend, "I totally bombed the test!" The listener in this case infers that the speaker couldn't have literally bombed the test but is using the phrase figuratively, and so he understands that the friend did poorly on the test. In similar ways, readers must make continual assessment of the written situation in order to infer meaning. So, for instance, if a student reads a chapter about the end of WWII, she might read that the Americans bombed Hiroshima and Nagasaki. In this case, of course, she must infer that the word *bomb* is being used literally, not figuratively. Among other aspects that discourse studies has showed us, then, is that we constantly infer meanings by contextualizing both what we hear and what we read.

In the first example above, any potential ambiguity is caused by the word "bombed," a metaphor. Other figures of speech, such as metonyms, personification, and hyperbole; certain slangs; and jargon may also create ambiguity, forcing the listener or reader, again, to make inferences. You've probably heard students complain, as they painstakingly made their way through a highly jargon-laden passage or perhaps a metaphor-filled sonnet, "Why didn't the author just write in plain English?!" Instructors can help to allay some of this frustration by increasing students' understanding of the purposes for such language usage and by pointing out that these forms are not limited to classroom texts but instead appear in everyone's daily discourse. Figure 5.2 illustrates just how frequently we use figures of speech. In other words, we are constantly making inferences about texts based upon the discourse situation that we're in, and we often employ language that is figurative, colloquial, or jargon-heavy. Making students aware of the process they already use to understand everyday discourse will enable them to apply this process in more challenging situations.

SUSAN: Pam's racing over to talk to me about something.
ED: Why doesn't she just buzz you?
SUSAN: Because it's about something that's hush-hush. Plus, she likes to swap gossip with me.
ED: OK, but I bet she stays all evening bending your ear.
SUSAN: I'll try to push her along, but meanwhile, don't be a grouch to her, sweetie, please.

Figure 5.2 Figures of Speech Are Frequently Used

FIGURATIVE LANGUAGE

While many people regard figurative language as a special language exclusively found in literary texts, cognitive linguists have argued that tropes actually make up a large part of our everyday discourse, and they suggest that humans often employ these tropes, such as metaphors, metonyms, personification, and so on, in order to describe and understand their worlds more clearly (Lakoff, 1993; Gibbs and Steen, 1999; Gibbs, 2008). Table 5.1 illustrates a few categories of common cultural metaphors. Although poets and other writers may employ unconventional figures to create extraordinary and unusual images, researchers have shown that in fact this type of trope occurs infrequently and that, instead, most figures in literature arise from conventional, ordinary ones of the kind employed by people in their daily conversations (Kövecses, 2010). This finding is important for your students for several reasons. First, knowing that literary texts rarely contain completely new or unusual figures of speech can reduce students' anxiety about less familiar genres, such as the sonnet, play, or essay, where these figures are likely to occur. Second, students can gain confidence in their reading capabilities if they become aware that all texts in English, including their own discourses, are likely to share many of the same or similar figures because they reflect similar human experience. Whenever a student tells someone, "You're in a *heap* of trouble," or when students yell at a football game, "*Fight*, team, *fight!*" they are using common figures of speech in order to get their ideas across. And their friends or others who are listening to them speak must in turn contextualize their words in order to create meaning. We all use figures of speech in our oral and written discourse, just as writers have done for centuries. Take, for instance, Jefferson's description in *The Declaration of Independence* of the King's offenses, which he describes as "a long *train* of abuses," or his assertion that in the

Table 5.1 Common American English Metaphors

Category of Metaphor	Example
Wealth	You're going to have to *earn* my trust.
	The plan is *rich* with possibilities.
	The group meeting produced a *wealth* of ideas.
Sports	Our company insists you be a *team player*.
	We'll make it special—the whole *nine yards*.
	She's obviously the best choice for the job—it's a *slam-dunk*!
Time	The *afternoon raced* by.
	He's living on *borrowed time*.
	I *lost a lot of time* today standing in line at the market.

face of these ills citizens should "*throw off* such Government." Without Jefferson's use of these vivid figures, *The Declaration* would be a much less memorable document.

The following exercise gets students thinking about uses of figurative language in their everyday lives. For review, students might like to consult Table 5.2, which describes common figures of speech.

Table 5.2 Common Figures of Speech

Figure of Speech	Example
Metaphor A word or phrase that is used to imply comparison with something that is different yet analogous enough to make sense	This book is *rich* with illustrations. It's a *no-win* situation.
Simile The comparison of one thing with another thing of a different kind, using *like* or *as*	He drove *like a mad man*. The timer sounds *like a bird chirping*.
Metonym A word used in place of another with which it is closely associated	The government bailout of *Detroit* seems to be working. *Wall Street* closed up today.
Hyperbole Exaggerated statements or claims not meant to be taken literally	I've told you *a hundred times* to stop climbing on the fence! She's been waiting *forever* for you.
Personification The attribution of human characteristics to something non-human	That plant *needs a good, long drink*. The *sad wallpaper* in that room is a real downer.
Euphemism An expression used to replace a blunt or harsh word with a milder word or expression	My brother is *between jobs* right now. The ladies' *restroom* is down the hall.

Standards

4. Interpret words and phrases as they are used in a text, including determining technical, connotative, and figurative meanings, and analyze how specific word choices shape meaning or tone.
5. Analyze the structure of texts, including how specific sentences, paragraphs, and larger portions of the text (e.g., a section, chapter, scene, or stanza) relate to each other and the whole.

EXERCISE 5.4

Ask students to pick out the common figures of speech in each of the following sentences and identify their meanings. The figures include instances of metaphor, metonym, personification, simile, euphemism, and hyperbole. Discuss with them how we are able to understand their usage: Why have these figures of speech developed? What in our culture or in our general human experience might have contributed to their creation? For example, we often hear the phrase, "Be a team player," in situations that have nothing to do with sports. The widespread use of the phrase, along with many other sports metaphors, reveals the significant place of sports in American life: most of us readily understand the context of words and phrases such as these, and yet someone from another country not immersed in sports may have a more difficult time comprehending their meaning.

1. *There's an all-out war between the two football teams.*
2. *That magazine ad screams for attention.*
3. *I have a million things to do, and you ask me now to take you to a friend's?*
4. *He's as nice as a penned-up pitbull.*
5. *The Principal's Office announced today that students would not be allowed off campus at lunchtime until further notice.*
6. *Hey, I just won again; I'm on a roll.*
7. *He's passed away.*
8. *The White House decided to hold off on promoting the new tax cut bill.*
9. *I'm starving! When do we eat?*
10. *My life is an open book.*

Guided Questions for Class Discussion

1. Ask students why a sports rivalry might be described as a "war." How do Americans feel about sports in our culture? What place do sports have?
2. Have students consider the effects of using hyperbole. Does it always achieve its desired effect? Can they think of a situation where the use of hyperbole would be inappropriate?
3. Ask students why the writer chose to use metonymy in Sentences #5 and #8. Why not mention more specifically who did these actions?

4. What images do the metaphors in Sentences #6 and #10 create in the reader's mind?

5. Have students discuss why many of us choose to use euphemisms, like that in Sentence #7. What would be another way of saying this with the same meaning?

Using Figurative Language

The examples of figures of speech in Exercise 5.4 should have been quite familiar to your students since they are commonly employed in our culture. Perhaps some of your students still protest, though, that they use only "straight speech," or plain writing, to get their ideas across and they wonder why anyone would resort to using language tropes. Ask your class to complete the following exercise in order to explore reasons why people might elect to use figurative language.

Standard

6. Assess how point of view or purpose shapes the content and style of a text.

EXERCISE 5.5

The following exercise presents sets of two sentences each, one sentence containing a figure of speech and the other sentence its "translation" in plain language without any figures. Ask your students to get into groups and read through the sets of sentences, identifying the figures of speech. Each group should then discuss the guided questions below.

1. a. *The roof is leaking again—it's a never ending problem.*
   b. *The roof repeatedly leaks.*
2. a. *She's as pretty as a model.*
   b. *She's really pretty.*
3. a. *The throne has decreed that Sir Thomas will die.*
   b. *King Henry said that Sir Thomas will die.*
4. a. *That plant is thirsty.*
   b. *That plant needs water.*
5. a. *I have a hole in my heart when you are gone.*
   b. *I miss you a lot.*
6. a. *These revenue enhancements will support the U.S. economy.*
   b. *The government's broke, so we're raising your taxes.*

Guided Questions for Class Discussion

1. What differences in effect on the listener/reader do the two sentences in each set have?
2. For each set of sentences, consider the meaning that is conveyed: how does the sentence with the figure of speech convey meaning differently from the sentence containing plain speech?
3. In what situations might figures of speech be preferred? In what situations might plain speech be more appropriate? How do the intended audience and purposes of the text, in other words the context, influence the use of figurative language?

As we note above, studies have shown that, contrary to some expectations, most poetic language is based upon common, ordinary metaphors and other figures of speech (Kövecses, 2010). Thus, while readers must make inferences when reading figurative language, it is likely that they are able to grasp the meaning because their experiences of human existence are probably very similar to those of the writer. The following two exercises show how readers can use their personal experiences and cultural knowledge to bring meaning to texts that employ figurative language.

Standards

6. Assess how point of view or purpose shapes the content and style of a text.
7. Integrate and evaluate content presented in diverse formats and media, including visually and quantitatively, as well as in words.

EXERCISE 5.6

In his famous poem "Ode on a Grecian Urn," John Keats employs a variety of figures of speech. Ask your students to read through the first two stanzas of the poem and identify the various figures, using Table 5.2 above if they wish. (You can find the poem at http://www.bartleby.com/101/625.html.) As a class, then discuss the stanzas, employing the guided questions listed below.

Guided Questions for Class Discussion

1. In a conventional ode, the speaker typically addresses something: a person, a thing, an idea. Ask your students whom or what the speaker is addressing.
2. The speaker uses two metaphors to describe the urn, calling it an "unravish'd bride of quietness" and "foster-child of Silence and slow Time." Explain to

your students that this is an ancient Greek stone or clay urn decorated with painted scenes of a girl being chased by wooers, of lovers under a tree, and of musicians. Once they learn of the scenes on the urn, ask them to consider whether the two metaphors appropriately describe the urn. Why is the urn "unravished"? And who are its parents, if it is indeed a "foster-child"? Who made this urn?

3. In the third line, the speaker uses another figure to again describe the urn: a "historian." Ask students to identify the type of figure and describe in what way the urn acts as an historian.

4. Have students identify the type of figure the speaker uses when he compares the urn's "tale" to "our rhyme."

5. Later on in the poem the speaker talks about pipes and timbrels making music and imagines the music as sweet, yet he notes that any music from these painted instruments must necessarily go "unheard." He then argues, though, that those tunes "unheard" are sweeter. Have your students discuss the meaning of this paradox. How can music be sweeter when unheard?

6. The speaker seems to find something positive about the fact that this scene is frozen in time on the urn. Ask your students why he might see this as positive. What happens to humans with the passage of time?

7. Ask your students to consider what Keats' poem would be like without the figures of speech. You might have them try to translate one or both stanzas into plain speech: what is the effect of this? Would the ideas conveyed be so memorable?

Figures of speech of course appear in informational texts as well. The following exercise asks students to read a familiar work by an author noted for his masterful use of such language.

EXERCISE 5.7

From *Walden; or, Life in the Woods*:

I went to the woods because I wished to live deliberately, to front only the essential facts of life, and see if I could not learn what it had to teach, and not, when I came to die, discover that I had not lived. I did not wish to live what was not life, living is so dear; nor did I wish to practise resignation, unless it was quite necessary. I wanted to live deep and suck out all the marrow of life, to live so sturdily and Spartan-like as to put to rout all that was not life, to cut a broad swath and shave close, to drive life into a corner, and reduce it to its lowest terms, and, if it proved to be mean, why then to get the whole and genuine meanness of it, and publish its meanness to the world; or if it were sublime, to know it by experience, and be able to give a true account of it in my next excursion. For most men, it appears to me, are in a strange uncertainty about it, whether it is of the devil or of God, and have somewhat hastily concluded that it is the chief end of man here to "glorify God and enjoy him forever."

(Thoreau, 1854, Where I lived and what I lived for, p. 16)

Guided Questions for Class Discussion

1. Ask your students to get into small groups and read through the passage. Point out that the third sentence of the passage contains a string of metaphors; ask each group to take each metaphor individually and write in their own words its meaning: students should agree on the meanings written. Then they should compare their language to Thoreau's: What differences in effects on the reader do they note between their writing and his?
2. Thoreau is explaining how he wishes to live life, and, by implication, is suggesting that the reader should live this way, too. Given the metaphors he employs, ask your students how Thoreau views "living." What does life become for a person who wishes to live as Thoreau does? Does anything in American culture promote this way of living?
3. Ask your students to identify what Thoreau means by "next excursion" at the end of the third sentence. What kind of figure is this?
4. Have students consider and discuss the use of figurative language in the passage: What would be the effect if it were written in plain speech? Would anyone still read it today? Why do Thoreau's metaphors make it memorable?

Exercise Extension

Have students read the following post from a blog that reviews new products in the gaming industry. Ask them to identify the figures of speech in the passage, noting down on paper which were used. Finally, have students write a paragraph on their reactions to reading this kind of language on this site: Is it expected? Unexpected? What does figurative language add, if anything, to the reader's understanding of the text?

From *Gaming Blog*:
Square Enix has taken the wraps off its latest action title for PS3 and Xbox 360, NIER. The game has been given an official website as well as an embedded trailer. The game is being developed by Cavia and its trailer gives a feeling that NIER may be on the lines of Devil May Cry, look-wise. The website says that NIER will require the players to don the shoes of an "unyielding protagonist" who is out to find a cure for his daughter as she battles against Black Scrawl virus. Apparently, the game will be your traditional hack n' slash bit, only spruced with an emotional plot. Check out some shadowy creatures facing the wrath of a really angry hero. NIER wields a sword like a toy and the official page says he's armed with multiple weapons and can weave magic. Ah, right up our alley it seems. We'll report more on the game from E3 as NIER is an official part of Square Enix's lineup at the event. And as the trailer says: Coming in 2010.

(Sharma, 2009)

SLANG AND JARGON

Another potential obstacle to reading comprehension is a text's use of specialized languages, such as slang or jargon. *Slang* is an informal discourse used by members of a particular community, typically a subset of a larger community, although some slangs are more widely employed, such as the slang used by U.S. teenagers, or that of hip hop artists. (See Figure 5.3.) Slang is designed to maintain the exclusivity of a group: it's an insider language that excludes all non-users. Slang often contains invented words and phrases, taboo words, and plays on words, all of which add to its distinctiveness.

Authors of both informational and literary texts frequently use slang to maintain authenticity in a work or to attract a particular audience, yet there are some risks involved in its use. For instance, Anthony Burgess' 1962 novel *A Clockwork Orange*, about a gang of punks in Britain, risked losing its readers, because of his use of an invented Russian-Anglo slang employed throughout, which made comprehension difficult. In a more recent example, David Macinnis Gill's YA novel, *Soul Enchilada*, was criticized by several readers on a review site for its heavy use of slang, which they claimed detracted from their reading experience. Yet some respondents to these latter criticisms wrote that they appreciated Gill's inclusion of the authentic slang.

Jargon is another kind of specialized language, but different from slang, jargon is usually associated with a particular profession, discipline, or area of study. Containing a specific vocabulary and perhaps even syntax, jargon exists so that members of a community can communicate efficiently and effectively. Like slang, jargon is an exclusive language, known only to those of a particular group.

While not all texts contain slang and jargon, many do, and so students should be aware of their uses and purposes. The following exercise asks students to analyze introductory paragraphs containing slang and/or jargon, taken from both literary and informational texts.

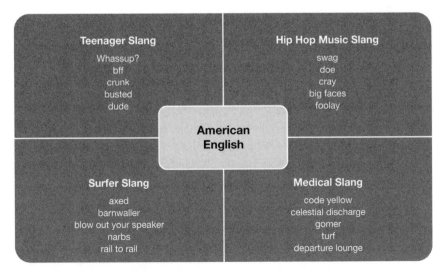

Figure 5.3 Examples of Slang Communities

Standards

8. Delineate and evaluate the argument and specific claims in a text, including the validity of the reasoning as well as the relevance and sufficiency of the evidence.
9. Analyze how two or more texts address similar themes or topics in order to build knowledge or to compare the approaches the authors take.

EXERCISE 5.8

Have students get into small groups and read the following passages taken from both literary and informational texts. Ask them to discuss the use of slang and jargon, following the guided questions below each passage.

A. From *The Catcher in the Rye*:

If you really want to hear about it, the first thing you'll probably want to know is where I was born, and what my lousy childhood was like, and how my parents were occupied and all before they had me, and all that David Copperfield kind of crap, but I don't feel like going into it, if you want to know the truth.

(Salinger, 1951, p. 1)

Guided Questions for Class Discussion

1. Ask students to identify the slang in the paragraph.
2. Have them consider the effect on the reader of the narrator's using words like "lousy" and "crap."
3. Ask them to discuss the tone of the passage. How does the narrator come across? What do they think the rest of the work might be about?
4. From 1961 to 1982 *The Catcher in the Rye* was the most censored book in high schools and libraries in the United States (American Library Association, 2012). Today, it is still often censored, especially in many school libraries and classrooms. Much of the criticism of the novel centers on its language, including the novel's inclusion of blasphemy, taboo words, and teen slang, all thought to have a corrupting influence on teenage readers who are the target audience for the book. Ask your students to consider this first paragraph of the novel: why might it have raised concerns for its readers in past decades, and why does it still bother some readers today?

B. From *Bronx Masquerade*:

I ain't particular about doing homework, you understand. My teachers practically faint whenever I turn something in. Matter of fact, I probably got the longest list of excuses for missing homework of anyone alive. Except for my homey Tyrone. He tries to act like he's not even interested in school, like there's no point in studying hard, or dreaming about tomorrow, or bothering to graduate. He's got his reasons. I keep on him about going to school, though, saying I need the company. Besides, I tell him, if he drops out and gets a J.O.B., he won't have any time to work on his songs. That always gets to him. Tyrone might convince everybody else that he's all through with dreaming, but I know he wants to be a big hip-hop star. He's just afraid he won't live long enough to do it. Me, I hardly ever think about checking out. I'm more worried about figuring what I want to do if I live.

(Grimes, 2001, p. 3)

Guided Questions for Class Discussion

1. Ask students to identify the slang in the passage—what common conventions of slang are being used?
2. The speaker in the passage is only identified by his/her language. What characteristics might your students assign this speaker? For instance, what age and gender do they think the speaker is, and how can they tell?
3. Ask your students what they think the rest of the book might be about. Based on their answers, ask them if they think the slang spoken by the speaker is appropriate.

C. From *Competition Rules: United States Surfing Championships*:
C.1 The judging criteria for AIR Division shall be:
The surfer who performs the most committed radical air in the most critical section of a wave with height, technical difficulty and control will maximize their scoring potential.

Note: Criteria rating (shall be based on 2′ to 3′ above the lip), all airs depend on height, bigger the air the higher the score, point rating below may vary depending on height, commitment and control as determined by wave conditions.

C.2	FRONTSIDE AIRS	
Type of Air	**Description**	**Rating**
Standard Air	Ollie	2–5
Double Grab	Both hands	2–5
Slob Air	Back hand grabbing toe-side Rail	5–7
Alley Oop	Off the lip of the wave	5–7
Lean Air	Front hand grabbing heel-side rail	6–8

(Surfusa.org, 2005)

Guided Questions for Class Discussion

1. Ask your students to identify the jargon used in the above passage. Have them find specifically the jargon that may have different meanings in another context. (For instance, the words *radical* or *lean* here may mean something very different from how they are usually employed.)
2. Have your students discuss the value of using jargon. What is its benefit? Given that these are contest rules, does it matter that they contain jargon? Shouldn't rules be stated as clearly as possible to prevent misunderstanding?
3. Slang and jargon possess many similarities. The rules above may contain both.

Ask your students to identify those words that may have originated as jargon but that now have become part of a slang language community.

D. From *Video Games Blogger.*

its amazing get it. Game plays smoothly, ill let u know if your hard core mariokart player its the best of the series yet. and as far as handhelds and consoles alike they fixed the drifting from nintendo ds that allowed u to hyper boost around the whole track (online this was tedious to keep up) and now its perfect, just a good drift gets u boost. and they brought back coins for top speed adding even more skill to the game which was a gba thing i liked. The tracks are awesome full of secrets and for me this mario kart isn't overdone with corkyness that i found with the wii.

(Eviltwin5559, 2011, Comments)

Guided Questions for Class Discussion

1. Ask students to identify both the slang terms and the jargon used in the blogger's post above. Do some of the terms overlap categories?
2. Is the jargon so technical that people outside the gaming world wouldn't understand it? Inquire if anyone in the students' groups found the post difficult to comprehend.
3. What are some of the stereotypical characteristics of gamers? Following the section in Chapter 1 on Language that discussed insiders and outsiders in language communities, are gamers typically conceived as outsiders or insiders within larger language communities such as school, work, and home? How difficult is it to become a member of a gamers' language community? Is this group typically more open or more closed to new people?

Standard

10. Read and comprehend complex literary and informational texts independently and proficiently.

EXERCISE 5.9

As we've shown through our discussion in this chapter, perhaps the most important factor in achieving meaning while reading is identifying context. Not having knowledge of the context of a written work makes it impossible for students to take the first steps towards comprehension, such as thinking about how their lives relate to the ideas presented, or why writers have made the language choices that they have. In this last exercise of the chapter, we ask students to analyze two short passages, using the concepts they've learned from doing the exercises throughout the chapter. Each passage is accompanied by two parts: a set of questions to guide class discussion, and then a written exercise.

Passage #1

Shakespeare's *Romeo and Juliet* is often assigned at the secondary level because the lead characters are teenagers, and so it is thought that high school students can relate to, or have insight into, the conflicts dramatized in the work. Act I introduces us to Romeo who has just been rejected by a girl he loves, and Juliet, who is so young that she hasn't yet thought about love and marriage. The two meet, woo one another, and fall in love despite their parents' objections. Although living in another time and place, today's students may have gone through experiences similar to those of Romeo and Juliet, albeit employing different language and behaviors. The following exercise asks students to consider the language Romeo and Juliet use to woo one another and to compare this language to that which they might employ today.

Give students a handout of the lines spoken by Romeo and Juliet in Act I, Scene 5 when they first meet. Ask them to read through it silently for initial comprehension and then discuss the lines as a class, using the questions below.

ROMEO (taking Juliet's hand):	*If I profane with my unworthiest hand*
	This holy shrine, the gentle sin is this:
	My lips, two blushing pilgrims, ready stand
	To smooth that rough touch with a tender kiss.
JULIET:	*Good pilgrim, you do wrong your hand too much,*
	Which mannerly division shows in this;
	For saints have hands that pilgrims' hands do touch,
	And palm to palm is holy palmers' kiss.
ROMEO:	*Have not saints lips, and holy palmers too?*
JULIET:	*Ay, pilgrim, lips that they must use in prayer.*
ROMEO:	*Oh then, dear saint, let lips do what hands do.*
	They pray; grant thou, lest fate turn to despair.
JULIET:	*Saints do not move, though grant for prayers' sake.*
ROMEO:	*Then move not while my prayer's effect I take.*
	(he kisses her)
	That from my lips, by thine, my sin is purged.
JULIET:	*Then have my lips the sin that they have took.*
ROMEO:	*Sin from my lips? O trespass sweetly urged.*
	Give me my sin again. (he kisses her)
JULIET:	*You kiss by th'book.*

(Act I, Scene 5, lines 104–122)

Part 1

Guided Questions for Class Discussion

1. Ask a student to summarize out loud the action of this scene: what is taking place?
2. Ask students what extended metaphor Romeo uses, helped by Juliet, in order to eventually kiss her lips. What does Romeo mean by describing his lips as "two blushing pilgrims"?

3. What does Juliet suggest that her lips have received from Romeo, and how does that open the possibility of another kiss?
4. What do students think Juliet means by telling Romeo that he "kissed by th' book"? Do we use this expression today—"by the book"? What meaning does it have?

Part 2

Have students work with a partner to "translate" this scene between Romeo and Juliet. How would such a scene be played out today between two teenagers meeting for the first time? Note that Romeo and Juliet meet at a party given by the Capulets (Romeo is let in only because he and his friends are in masks). Where might such a meeting take place today? Have students set the scene, or describe the setting, before they write the lines for the characters. Ask them to think about contemporary language that would be used today between teens as they write their scripts. What level of formality would it have? How casual? How slangy? Once students have written their scenes, ask them to act them out in front of the class and have other class members compare the script with the play, discussing the differences and similarities between the emotions expressed, formality of the language, forwardness and friendliness of the encounter, and so on.

Passage #2

Letter from Birmingham Jail was handwritten in 1963 while Dr. King was imprisoned in the Birmingham jail, after being arrested for his part in a non-violent protest against racial segregation in Birmingham, AL. The letter was addressed to the local white clergy in Birmingham who recognized that racial inequality existed but argued that all efforts to change such inequality should come through changing the laws, and thus solely through the courts and not through public demonstration. King disagreed with such an approach. Briefly review with your students some of the public outcry in the 1960s over the topic of civil rights: the marches, the Freedom Riders, sit-ins, protests, violence, assassinations, and federally mandated integration. Then ask your students to read or re-read the 12th paragraph of Dr. King's *Letter from Birmingham Jail*, which begins with the frequently quoted metaphor "stinging darts of segregation." You can find the entire letter at http://www.mlkonline. net/jail.html. The following discussion questions and writing activity ask students to analyze the language King uses in his persuasive appeal.

Part 1

Guided Questions for Class Discussion

1. Ask students to identify the main point of this paragraph.
2. Ask students to count the number of sentences in this paragraph (4). How is the second sentence structured, that is, what makes it so much longer than the other three? How many figures of speech can your students identify in this single sentence?
3. Teachers frequently caution students to use figures of speech in a limited fashion; too many can be confusing and even ridiculous in their excess. Has Dr. King erred in using more than one figure of speech in a single sentence?

4. Remind your students that Dr. King is writing to persuade people to support the actions of the civil rights movement, not just addressing those who already agree with him. How do they think readers unfamiliar with Dr. King might have responded to this paragraph? What sort of effect does this language have?

5. We usually think of logic and facts as being the most convincing type of evidence when persuading an audience. Why didn't Dr. King provide facts and statistics about the harm segregation was causing in the United States?

Part 2

Divide the class into small groups of three or four students, and then ask them to "translate" Dr. King's paragraph into completely literal sentences. They should remove all figures of speech and create an objective tone by using *he* and *she* rather than *you* and *your* for the pronouns. After they finish, ask one student to read the original version and another student to read his/her group's translation. Which one does the class find to be more persuasive? Why?

Exercise Extension

Another way that authors deliberately manipulate audiences for a particular effect can be seen in the use of constructed languages, languages that have been consciously created and thus not developed naturally. Constructed languages include Elvish and others in J. R. R. Tolkien's *Lord of the Rings* trilogy; the Na'vi language from the film *Avatar*; and the Dothraki language from George R. R. Martin's novel *Game of Thrones*.

Ask your students to research these texts on-line, or find them in the library, and bring to class examples of the constructed languages. (You may use other texts as well: novels of H. P. Lovecraft, Ursula Le Guin, Stephen King, Jules Verne, and the Harry Potter series, as well as the TV shows *Land of the Lost*, *Star Trek*, and others all contain constructed languages.) Have students read through the language examples they've brought into class and then think about their inclusion in these texts. Why do they think the author has gone to so much trouble to create these languages? What effects do the languages have on the over-all narrative of the work? What effect does the constructed language have on the reader: what is his reading experience of the text?

MEETING STUDENTS WHERE THEY ARE

In an editorial for "ESPN Commentary," L. Z. Granderson (2010) calls on coaches and athletes to stop using figures of speech that compare sports activities to war and violence. His comments were motivated by a Tennessee football coach who, in the excitement of a post-game press conference, compared his team's poor performance to the German army's weak response to the Allied invasion of Normandy during World War II. Although this particular coach was a bit extreme, the language of sports and the language of war frequently overlap. Players call themselves "soldiers" and "warriors," even though they're not risking their lives to protect others. Teams are encouraged to "kill" their opponents. Football teams respond to "bombs," and basketball players "shoot" field goals. Granderson acknowledges that such language is intended to inspire participants and fans, but sees it as being misleading, even disrespectful, to the real members of the armed forces, who aren't playing games. He also worries that it desensitizes users to the presence of real violence and physical danger. Others, though, find the connection to be natural because of the intense individual pressure each individual feels and they see no disrespect in using the same language to describe the activities of both sports and war. Ask your students, either individually or in groups, to list as many figures of speech as they can that draw parallels between sports games and war or violence. Then ask them to write a brief response that takes a position on this topic: do they personally find such language troubling?

Guided Questions for Class Discussion

1. Have your students heard this use of metaphoric language in sports that they've personally been involved in? Or is it just used in professional sports? How typical is it?
2. The NBA Commissioner, David Stern, recently condemned a Nike print ad that portrayed Kobe Bryant and LeBron James as warriors in scaly armor, about to do battle on the court. In the ad, both players use references to guns and gunplay when describing the court action. The ad was subsequently pulled from circulation. What are your students' feelings about these actions? Was the NBA right to criticize the ad? Was Nike right to pull it? Can language be harmful or dangerous?

LOOKING TO THE FUTURE

In this chapter we've talked about the necessary contextualizing that all readers do in order to infer meaning, and we've noted how unfamiliar contexts, including historic times, foreign places, and language usages can pose special problems for readers. The fact that language is in a constant state of change increases the potential for readers' problems with comprehension; terms used in other places and times may be completely foreign to our students today. Just think about the slang terms, for example, that were used in previous centuries: would students reading texts from these time periods be able to recognize terms like *bridewell* (19th-century British term for "prison"), *bill and coo, from nowhere, mirror warmer, groovy*, and so on? Jargon, too, becomes rapidly dated: who uses the term *kelvinator* to describe a refrigerator today or who would talk about *cathode ray tubes* when discussing TV reception? As a recent on-line description of a cathode tube notes, this is a "dead technology," which means that the terms that make up its name are also dead, or at least passé.

For this exercise, ask your students to think about the slang and jargon they use today and then write down some examples of it. Have them consider the various contexts in which they use slang and jargon, so they can have several examples: slang they use on-line or when using other forms of technology (bbl, flame, OMG, etc.), slang they use with friends (cool, busted, crunk, emo, etc.), jargon they employ when performing a particular task or activity (four-top, in the weeds, noob, leet, beta, yard sale, etc.). Now ask them to imagine historians 200 years in the future discovering recordings of their speech. Will these future listeners be able to understand the slang? Why or why not? What sort of contextual changes would make their everyday language difficult to understand? Have them write a one-page essay in which they explore the answer to this question, to be handed in and/or to be shared with the rest of the class.

SUGGESTED FURTHER READING

Reading Comprehension Research

Barton, D., Hamilton, M., and Ivanic, R. (Eds.) (2000). *Situated literacies*. New York: Routledge. This is a collection of key writings from leading international scholars in the field of literacy. Each contribution makes the link between literacies in specific contexts and broader social practices. Topics include the functions of literacies in shaping and sustaining identities in communities of practice, and the relationship between texts and the practices associated with their use of the role of discourse analysis in literacy studies.

Kamil, M. L., Pearson, P. D., Moje, E. B., and Afflerbach, P. (Eds.) (2010). *Handbook of reading research*, Vol. 4. New York: Routledge. This volume is a review of topics and themes in reading research literature conducted since Vol. 3 was issued in 2000.

Linguistics and Literature

Gerbig, A. and Müller-Wood, A. (2006). Introduction: Conjoining linguistics and literature. *College English 33*(2) (Spring), 85–90. This article introduces a special issue of *College English* dedicated to the topic of literature and linguistics. The editors briefly describe several ways, expanded upon later in the issue's articles, in which this intersection provides fruitful and interesting approaches to performing literary analysis, analyzing style, teaching metaphor, and other topics.

Traugott, E. C. and Pratt, M. L. (1980). *Linguistics: For students of literature*. New York: Harcourt, Brace, Jovanovich. One of the first works written on the intersection of linguistics and literature, this text provides clear explanations for applying linguistic concepts to the study of literature.

Language and Literature in Secondary Teaching

Denham, K. and Lobeck, A. (Eds.) (2005). *Language in the schools: Integrating linguistic knowledge into K-12 teaching*. Mahwah, NJ: Lawrence Erlbaum. This text focuses on how basic linguistic knowledge can inform teachers' approaches to language issues in the multicultural, linguistically diverse classroom.

Luria, H., Seymour, D. M., and Smoke, T. (Eds.) (2006). *Language and linguistics in context: Readings and applications for teachers*. Mahwah, NJ: Lawrence Erlbaum. Designed to be used in a range of courses in English language arts teacher education programs, this text brings together a variety of readings that provide valuable insights into the relationship between language and language study and educational policies, literacy, and pedagogy.

College and Career Readiness Anchor Standards of the Common Core State Standards for English Language Arts

College and Career Readiness Anchor Standards for Language

Conventions of Standard English

1. Demonstrate command of the conventions of standard English grammar and usage when writing or speaking.
2. Demonstrate command of the conventions of standard English capitalization, punctuation, and spelling when writing.

Knowledge of Language

3. Apply knowledge of language to understand how language functions in different contexts, to make effective choices for meaning or style, and to comprehend more fully when reading or listening.

Vocabulary Acquisition and Use

4. Determine or clarify the meaning of unknown and multiple-meaning words and phrases by using context clues, analyzing meaningful word parts, and consulting general and specialized reference materials, as appropriate.
5. Demonstrate understanding of figurative language, word relationships, and nuances in word meanings.
6. Acquire and use accurately a range of general academic and domain-specific words and phrases sufficient for reading, writing, speaking, and listening at the college and career readiness level; demonstrate independence in gathering vocabulary knowledge when considering a word or phrase important to comprehension or expression.

(p. 51)

College and Career Readiness Anchor Standards for Speaking and Listening

Comprehension and Collaboration

1. Prepare for and participate effectively in a range of conversations and collaborations with diverse partners, building on others' ideas and expressing their own clearly and persuasively.
2. Integrate and evaluate information presented in diverse media and formats, including visually, quantitatively, and orally.
3. Evaluate a speaker's point of view, reasoning, and use of evidence and rhetoric.

Presentation of Knowledge and Ideas
4. Present information, findings, and supporting evidence such that listeners can follow the line of reasoning and the organization, development, and style are appropriate to task, purpose, and audience.
5. Make strategic use of digital media and visual displays of data to express information and enhance understanding of presentations.
6. Adapt speech to a variety of contexts and communicative tasks, demonstrating command of formal English when indicated or appropriate.

(p. 48)

College and Career Readiness Anchor Standards for Writing

Text Types and Purposes★
1. Write arguments to support claims in an analysis of substantive topics or texts, using valid reasoning and relevant and sufficient evidence.
2. Write informative/explanatory texts to examine and convey complex ideas and information clearly and accurately through the effective selection, organization, and analysis of content.
3. Write narratives to develop real or imagined experiences or events using effective technique, well-chosen details, and well-structured event sequences.

Production and Distribution of Writing
4. Produce clear and coherent writing in which the development, organization, and style are appropriate to task, purpose, and audience.
5. Develop and strengthen writing as needed by planning, revising, editing, rewriting, or trying a new approach.
6. Use technology, including the Internet, to produce and publish writing and to interact and collaborate with others.

Research to Build and Present Knowledge
7. Conduct short as well as more sustained research projects based on focused questions, demonstrating understanding of the subject under investigation.
8. Gather relevant information from multiple print and digital sources, assess the credibility and accuracy of each source, and integrate the information while avoiding plagiarism.
9. Draw evidence from literary or informational texts to support analysis, reflection, and research.

Range of Writing
10. Write routinely over extended time frames (time for research, reflection, and revision) and shorter time frames (a single sitting or a day or two) for a range of tasks, purposes, and audiences.

(p. 41)

★These broad types of writing include many subgenres.

College and Career Readiness Anchor Standards for Reading

Key Ideas and Details
1. Read closely to determine what the text says explicitly and to make logical inferences from it; cite specific textual evidence when writing or speaking to support conclusions drawn from the text.
2. Determine central ideas or themes of a text and analyze their development; summarize the key supporting details and ideas.
3. Analyze how and why individuals, events, and ideas develop and interact over the course of a text.

Craft and Structure
4. Interpret words and phrases as they are used in a text, including determining technical, connotative, and figurative meanings, and analyze how specific word choices shape meaning or tone.
5. Analyze the structure of texts, including how specific sentences, paragraphs, and larger portions of the text (e.g., a section, chapter, scene, or stanza) relate to each other and the whole.
6. Assess how point of view or purpose shapes the content and style of a text.

Integration of Knowledge and Ideas
7. Integrate and evaluate content presented in diverse formats and media, including visually and quantitatively, as well as in words.
8. Delineate and evaluate the argument and specific claims in a text, including the validity of the reasoning as well as the relevance and sufficiency of the evidence.
9. Analyze how two or more texts address similar themes or topics in order to build knowledge or to compare the approaches the authors take.

Range of Reading and Level of Text Complexity
10. Read and comprehend complex literary and informational texts independently and proficiently.

(p. 35)

References

Aitchison, J. (2003). *Words in the mind: An introduction to the mental lexicon* (3rd ed.). Chichester, UK: Wiley-Blackwell.

Akmajian, A., Demers, R. A., Farmer, A. K., and Harnish, R. M. (2010). *Linguistics: An introduction to language and communication* (6th ed.). Cambridge, MA: MIT Press.

American Library Association. (2012). Banned and/or challenged books from the Radcliffe Publishing Course Top 100 Novels of the 20th Century. Retrieved January 5, 2012 from http://www.ala.org/ala/issuesadvocacy/banned/frequently challenged/challengedclassics/reasonsbanned/index.cfm.

Anderson, R. C., Reynolds, R. E., Schallert, D. L., and Goetz, E. T. (1977). Frameworks for comprehending discourse. *American Educational Research Journal, 14*, 367–381.

Andrews, L. (2006). *Language exploration and awareness: A resource book for teachers* (3rd ed.). Mahwah, NJ: Lawrence Erlbaum Associates.

Appleman, D. (2009). *Critical encounters in high school English: Teaching literary theory to adolescents* (2nd ed.). New York: Teachers College, Columbia University.

Assembling and operating Duke's Meade LX200GPS SCT. (n.d.). Retrieved January 7, 2012 from http://www.cgtp.duke.edu/~plesser/observatory/LX200GPS%20 Assembly.htm.

Boice, M. (1998). Chonic illness in adolescence. *Adolescence 33*(132), 927–941.

Brown, G. and Yule, G. (1983). *Discourse analysis.* Cambridge: Cambridge University Press.

Brownell, J. (2009). *Listening: Attitudes, principles, and skills* (4th ed.). Boston: Allyn and Bacon.

Campbell, M. (2003). Generic names for soft drinks by county. Retrieved January 30, 2012 from http://popvssoda.com/countystats/total-county.html.

Centers for Disease Control and Prevention (2006). Youth risk behavior surveillance – United States, 2005. *Morbidity and Mortality Weekly Report 55*(SS-5), 1–108.

Denham, K. and Lobeck. A. (Eds.) (2005). *Language in the schools: Integrating linguistic knowledge into K-12 teaching.* Mahwah, NJ: Lawrence Erlbaum Associates.

Devitt, A. (1993). Generalizing about genre: New conceptions of an old concept. *College Composition and Communication 44*(4), 573–586.

Dunn, P. A. and Lindblom, K. (2005). Developing savvy writers by analyzing grammar rants. In K. Denham and A. Lobeck (Eds.), *Language in the schools: Integrating linguistics knowledge into K-12 teaching* (pp. 191–208). Mahwah, NJ: Lawrence Erlbaum Associates.

Early, M. and Ericson, B. O. (1993). The act of reading. In L. M. Cleary and M. D. Linn (Eds.), *Linguistics for teachers* (pp. 313–324). New York: McGraw-Hill.

Emerson, R. W. (1844). Essays: Second series. Retrieved January 12, 2012 from http://www.emersoncentral.com/.

Eviltwin5559. (2011, December 2). Comments. How to unlock all Mario Kart 7 characters, vehicles, and tracks. *Video Games Blogger.* Retrieved January 13, 2012 from http://www.videogamesblogger.com/2011/12/02/how-to-unlock-all-mario-kart-7-characters-vehicles-tracks.htm#ixzz1jNcmJtIO.

Fodor, J. D. (1983). *Modularity in language.* Cambridge, MA: MIT Press.

Freeman, D. E. and Freeman, Y. S. (2004). *Essential linguistics: What you need to know to teach reading, ESL, spelling, phonics, and grammar.* Portsmouth, NH: Heinemann.

Garrett, M. F. (1988). Processes in language production. In F. J. Newmeyer (Ed.), *Linguistics: The Cambridge survey; III. Language: Psychological and biological aspects* (pp. 69–96). Cambridge: Cambridge University Press.

Gerbig, A. and Müller-Wood, A. (Eds.) (2006). *How globalization affects the teaching of English: Studying culture through texts.* Ceredigion, UK: Edwin Mellen.

Gibbs, R. W. (Ed.). (2008). *The Cambridge handbook of metaphor and thought.* Cambridge: Cambridge University Press.

Gibbs, R. W. and Steen, G. (Eds.) (1999). *Metaphor in cognitive linguistics: Selected papers from the fifth international cognitive linguistics conference.* Amsterdam, 1997. Amsterdam: John Benjamins.

Goddard, C. (1998). *Semantic analysis.* Oxford: Oxford University Press.

Goodman, K. (1996). *On reading.* Portsmouth, NH: Heinemann.

Goodman, Y. (2003). *Valuing language study: Inquiry into language for elementary and middle schools.* Urbana, IL: NCTE.

Granderson, L. Z. (2010, October 31). Sports teams are not at war. Retrieved January 2, 2012 from http://sports.espn.go.com/espn/commentary/news/story?id=5741408.

Grimes, N. (2001). *Bronx masquerade* (Excerpt). New York: Dial Books. Retrieved January 13, 2012 from Powell's Books, http://www.powells.com/biblio?show=HARDCOVER:NEW:9780803725690:16.99&page=excerpt.

Grognet, A. and Van Duzer, C. (2000). Listening skills in the workplace. Spring Institute for Intercultural Learning, 1–5. Retrieved January 5, 2012 from ELT Resource and Publications Library database on the World Wide Web: http://www.spring institute.org/index.php?action=publications&act=list&sort=header.

Halliday, M. A. K. (1985). *Spoken and written language.* Oxford: Oxford University Press.

Hazen, K. (2001). *Teaching about dialects* (Resource No. EDO-FL-01-04). Washington, DC: Center for Applied Linguistics.

Hudley, A. H. C. and Mallinson, C. (2010). *Understanding English language variation in schools.* New York: Teachers College Press.

Janks, H. (2005). Language and the design of texts. *English Teaching: Practice and Critique* 4(3), 97–110.

Joos, M. (1961). *The five clocks.* New York: Harcourt, Brace and World.

Knestrict, T. and Schoensteadt, L. (2005). Teaching social register and code-switching in the classroom. *Journal of Children and Poverty* 11(2), 177–185. doi:10.1080/1079 6120500195774.

Kotter, J. P. (1982) What effective general managers really do. *Harvard Business Review* 60, 156–167.

Kövecses, Z. (2010). *Metaphor.* New York: Oxford University Press.

Krenitsky-Korn, S. (2011). High school students with asthma: Attitudes about school health, absenteeism, and its impact on academic achievement. *Pediatric Nursing* 37(2), 61–68.

Lakoff, G. (1993). The contemporary theory of metaphor. In A. Ortonay (Ed.), *Metaphor and Thought* (pp. 202–251). Cambridge: Cambridge University Press.

Levitt, S. and Dubner, S. (2009). *Freakonomics: A rogue economist explores the hidden side of everything.* New York: William Morrow.

Lincoln, A. (1863). Draft of the Gettysburg Address: Nicolay Copy. Transcribed and annotated by the Lincoln Studies Center, Knox College, Galesburg, Illinois. Available at Abraham Lincoln Papers at the Library of Congress, Manuscript Division (Washington, DC: American Memory Project, [2000–02]), http://memory.loc.gov/ammem/alhtml/malhome.html.

Lovejoy, K. B. (2003). Practical pedagogy for composition. In G. Smitherman and V. Villanueva (Eds.), *Language diversity in the classroom: From intention to practice* (pp. 89–109). Carbondale: Southern Illinois University Press.

Martin, J. R. (2009). Genre and language learning: A social semiotic perspective. *Linguistics and Education: An International Research Journal 20*(1), 10–21. doi: 10.1016/j.linged.2009.01.

McPhee, J. (1991). *Coming into the country*. New York: Farrar, Straus, Giroux.

National Commission on Writing. (2004). Writing: A ticket to work or a ticket out: A survey of business leaders. Retrieved January 8, 2012 from http://www.college board.com/prod_downloads/writingcom/writing-ticket-to-work.

National Governors Association Center for Best Practices and Council of Chief State School Officers. (2010). *Common core state standards*. Retrieved January 30, 2012 from http://www.corestandards.org/.

NCTE. (1974). Students' right to their own language. *College Composition and Communication 25*(Fall), 1–32, Special Issue.

NCTE. (2008). *The NCTE definition of 21st century literacies*. Retrieved January 5, 2012 from http://www.ncte.org/positions/statements/21stcentdefinition.

Payne, R. (2008). Nine powerful practices. *Educational Leadership 65*(7), 48–52.

Purdy, M. and Borisoff, D. (1996). *Listening in everyday life: A personal and professional approach* (2nd ed.). Lanham, MD: University Press of America.

Redd, T. M. and Webb, K. S. (2005). *A teacher's introduction to African American English: What a writing teacher should know*. Urbana, IL: NCTE.

Renkema, J. (2004). *Introduction to discourse studies*. Amsterdam: John Benjamins.

Rosenblatt, L. (2005). *Making meaning with texts: Selected essays*. Portsmouth, NH: Heinemann.

Salinger, J. D. (1951). *The catcher in the rye* (reissue edition, 2001). New York: Back Bay Books.

Shakespeare, W. (1992). *Romeo and Juliet*. B. A. Mowat and P. Werstine (Eds.). New York: Washington Square-Pocket.

Sharma, G. (2009, May 31). NIER wields a bloody sword. *Gaming Blog*. Retrieved January 13, 2012 from http://www.gamingblog.org/entry/trailer-nier-wields-a-bloody-sword/.

Steffensen, M. S., Joag-Dev, C., and Anderson, R. (1979). A cross-cultural perspective on reading comprehension. *Reading Research Quarterly 15*(1), 10–29.

Strother, D. B. (1987). Practical applications of research: On listening. *Phi Delta Kappan 68*(8), 625–628.

Surfusa.org. (2005). *Competition rules*. Retrieved January 7, 2012 from http://www.surfusa.org/id3.html.

Surging Revs finally beat Patriots: York scored its first victory of the season against Somerset with Tuesday's 4–1 triumph. (2010, June 2). *York Daily Record*. Retrieved January 7, 2012 from http://www.ydr.com.

Swales, J. (1981). *Aspects of article introductions*. Birmingham: Aston University Language Studies Unit.

Thoreau, H. D. (1854). *Walden; or, life in the woods*. Boston: Ticknor and Fields. Retrieved January 12, 2012 from Project Gutenberg: http://www.gutenberg.org/etext/#205.

Trudgill, P. (1983). *On dialect: Social and geographical perspectives*. Oxford: Basil Blackwell.

United States Department of Health and Human Services. (1996). *The health insurance portability and accountability act of 1996 (HIPAA) privacy and security rule.* Retrieved January 6, 2012 from http://www.hhs.gov/ocr/privacy/.

Weaver, C. and Bush, J. (2008). *Grammar to enrich and enhance writing.* Portsmouth, NH: Heinemann.

Wesley, K. (2000). The ill effects of the five paragraph theme. *The English Journal 90*(1), 57–60.

Wetherall, M., Taylor, S., and Yates, S. (2001). *Discourse theory and practice: A reader.* London: Sage.

Wheeler, R. (2002). From home speech to school speech: Vantages on reducing the achievement gap in inner city schools. *Virginia English Bulletin 51*(2), 4–16.

Wheeler, R. (2005). Contrastive analysis and codeswitching: How and why to use the vernacular to teach standard English. In K. Denham, and A. Lobeck (Eds.), *Language in the schools: Integrating linguistic knowledge into K-12 teaching* (pp. 171–180). Mahwah, NJ: Lawrence Erlbaum Associates.

Wheeler, R. and Swords, R. (2006). *Code-switching: Teaching standard English in urban classrooms.* Urbana, IL: NCTE.

Wheeler, R. and Swords, R. (2010). *Code-switching lessons: Grammar strategies for linguistically diverse writers.* Portsmouth, NH: Heinemann.

Wible, S. (2006). Pedagogies of the "Students' Right" era: The language curriculum research group's project for linguistic diversity. *CCC 57*(3), 442–478.

Wilkinson, C. and Bretzing, R. (2011). High school girls' perceptions of selected fitness activities. *Physical Educator 68*(2), 58–65.

Wolfram, W. (1993). Teaching the grammar of vernacular English. In A. W. Glowka and D. M. Lance (Eds.), *Language variation in North American English: Research and teaching* (pp. 16–28). Washington, DC: Modern Language Association of America.

Wolfram, W. (2004). Social varieties of American English. In E. Finegan and J. R. Rickford (Eds.), *Language in the USA* (pp. 58–75). New York: Cambridge University Press.

Wolvin, A. and Coakley, G. (1988). *Listening* (revised ed.). Daybook, IA: William C. Brown.

Wyatt-Smith, C. (1997). Teaching and assessing writing: An Australian perspective. *English in Education 31*(3), 8–22.

Index

Locators in **bold** refer to figures and tables